"Sailing is my life."

ISBN: 146811042X
ISBN-13: 978-1468110425

Acknowledgements

This book was conceived as a self-published project. And so it is. But we encourage you to pass on word of *Chasing the Wind* to your friends, for in many respects Ernie Coleman's story is a beautiful and useful thing.

Chasing the Wind would not have been possible without Ernie Coleman. It is not easy, at age 93, to discuss the chapters of your life, and then watch them become chapters in a book. Because not all of those chapters have a happy ending.

Chasing the Wind would also not be possible without the cooperation of Ernie's family, who have supported him throughout, and provided valuable material. And you will meet them all in the pages to follow. Ernie's stepdaughter, Julie Lockner, was particularly key to the process. She proposed the idea, and saw it through from start to finish.

The writer would like to thank his wife, Margaret, whose quilts tell stories themselves. And their dog Abilene, who led long, contemplative walks through the woods. The writer would also like to thank his large circle of creative and inspiring friends: musicians, artists, photographers, writers, editors, bartenders, mothers and assorted gadflies. Be it an idea or just a word, you're all in here as well.

On the cover, Ernie Coleman is at the helm of *Desire* in the late 1990s, during a Scotch Bonnet Race on Lake Ontario. The photo was taken by John Altman.

Chasing the Wind was first published in March, 2012.

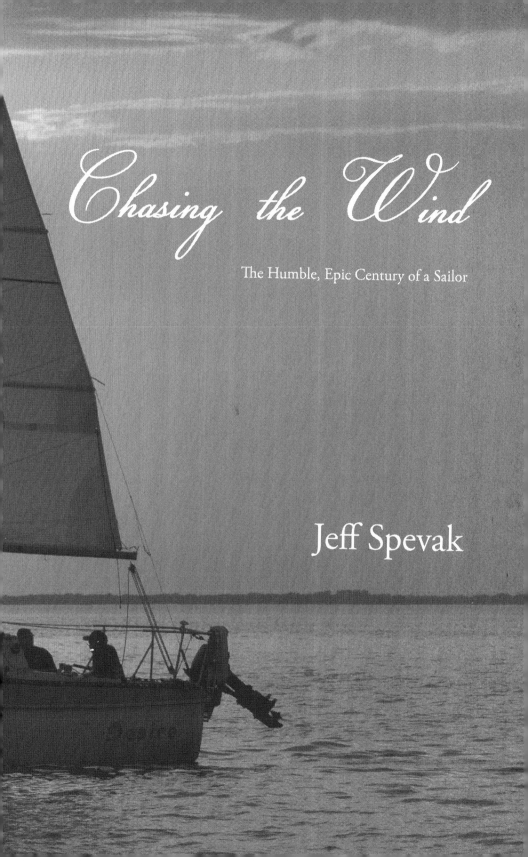

Chasing the Wind

The Humble, Epic Century of a Sailor

Jeff Spevak

Chapter One

It is 91 steps to the top of El Castillo, in the midst of the ancient ruins of Chichen Itza. Add up the steps on each of the four sides, plus the platform at the top, and it comes to 365. One step for each day of a year in any man's life. And as both the steps and the years add up, the climb gets more difficult. "I got to the top and – foof! – I collapsed," the old guy says. Fellow tourists rushed up to him. Are you all right?

"'Leave me alone,' I told them. I just lay there for a few minutes."

He was not concerned that he might die there, at the top of a Mayan pyramid, although perhaps such a climb in the Mexican sun was not the wisest expenditure of time for a man who was then 82 years old. His element is water. Ernie Coleman sails, an amateur racer who has filled his home with decades of trophies. His boat wasn't always the naturally swiftest on Lake Ontario. But Ernie knew all of the tricks that could ease his craft over the finish line first, especially on days when the wind was elusive.

Now Ernie is 93 and a little battered, but moves about easily enough, thanks to a few new parts here and there. And he is crisp of mind, as he is prodded for the details of his life. A man who was been caught up in the midst of life's largest moments. A child of the Great Depression. A graduate of the Greatest Generation, as we call it now. A carpenter, Ernie has built things, and rebuilt his life repeatedly, struggling through divorce and the death of two wives. With the marriages came one adopted child, seven step kids. He has adapted to change. He is a survivor.

A large part of the appeal of Ernie's story is that so many of us know a man or woman like him – a grandfather, or a more-distant aunt – but we don't know their stories. Some of these stories are modest life lessons. Others are remarkable adventures. In a metaphor that any sailor can relate to, each episode of Ernie's life can be thought of as a strand; when wound together, the strands create a strong rope. Or a line, as sailors prefer to call it, that he has unconsciously relied on in times of crisis.

The Navy had taken him out to see the world, first for World War II, then the Korean War. He didn't always like what he'd seen. Maui? "It was so perfect, it was monotonous." And he does not think of the Solomon Islands. Ernie's a short man, having lost a few inches to age, but broad-shouldered, with the large, knotted hands of his trade, carpentry. His hands wave in front of him for a moment, as though he's pushing away that memory of the Battle of Savo Island, during the Guadalcanal campaign. One-third of his shipmates, more than 300 men, were killed when the *USS Vincennes* rolled over in the early morning darkness and went to Iron Bottom Sound. So named because it is the graveyard of so many ships, and their crews. It is not a story he shares. "I know why those kids come back from Afghanistan and shoot themselves," he says sadly one morning, sitting on the shady patio at his home. "You lay awake at night, reacting, reacting, reacting. Because it's so real."

He exchanges those nightmares for beautiful evenings chasing the wind off the coast of Lake Ontario.

In his eighth decade, at an age when most men are settling down in front of the television to wait for the end, Ernie was still sailing. But the waters were increasingly uncharted. He'd climbed those 91 steps on that day in 1998 because he was trying to impress the woman he was courting. Marilyn, 25 years his junior. A travel agent who was showing him the world, watching to see if he could keep up. He could. Now he had been to Rome several times, examining ancient aqueducts with his builder's eye. Sailing in the Caribbean on a five-masted clipper ship, "Four hundred feet long," Marilyn says. "Four hundred and 39 feet," Ernie corrects. The captain had even let him handle the wheel for a while. Tourists were taking pictures of Ernie, as though they'd just come across one of those water-skiing squirrels. Marilyn had also taken him snow skiing for the first time, when he was 80. "After six lessons, I was skiing with her," Ernie insists. "In fact, I was holding back."

"No, you weren't," Marilyn chides him.

"You're a pleasure skier," Ernie says. He is a competitor. He chased Marilyn, and he caught her. "This guy's really elderly," she remembers thinking when she first met him. She'd placed an ad in the personals section of the newspaper, seeking a man who liked sailing and travel. She checked out 27 respondents. He was the 28th. Now they were married, living in the Madison Terrace house Ernie rebuilt just a couple of hundred yards from Lake Ontario Beach. A house with a small window facing north. He can look out that window every morning to see what's happening on Lake Ontario. The view changes every day.

But first, he had to get off of that Mexican pyramid. His fellow tourists were worried that he was dying at Chichen Itza, while he marveled at how, standing at one pyramid in the ruined complex, "you holler and get seven echoes." And "the sacrificial pool, where they threw the maidens." And the precision of the architecture, functioning as a giant stone calendar, the sheer size of the project allowing him to dismiss the fact that "they were off a little."

Ernie was off a little himself. The shortness of breath? The first signs of congenital heart disease. A stent would later help take care of that. "I caught my breath, and I was OK," he says. Then he got up, and walked down the pyramid.

Hope, the Thames River sailing barge owned by Ernie Coleman's grandparents.

Chapter Two

The color of your hair and eyes, the shape of your ears, and perhaps how long you will live, is encoded in genes buried in your body, in long strands of deoxyribonucleic acid. DNA. It is the basic instruction of your life. Somewhere within the double helixes of Ernie Coleman's DNA, mixed among the genes for woodworking, are powerful genes of sailing. Genes that lead him instinctively to water, complete with hardwiring for reading the wind, finding the good air.

These genes, Ernie muses, were handed down to him by his grandparents. For many years, in the late 1800s and early part of the 20th century, George and Clara Coleman owned a Thames sailing barge. A flat-bottomed boat designed to haul coal, mud, bricks or grain along the Thames estuary. From what Ernie has learned, George and Clara's boat, named *Hope*, was about 70 feet long, a little smaller than the norm for such a vessel, with a spritsail rigging that maximized maneuverability on the crowded Thames, while still allowing the couple to sail back and forth from London to Liverpool. "It was rigged in such a way," Ernie says, "when they came to a bridge, the mast folded down, they glided under, and cranked it back up."

It could not have been peaceful sailing, at least when loading or unloading the boat. In *London: The Biography*, Peter Ackroyd describes the Thames riverside as "filled with the sound of carts, horses, cranes and human voices, mingling with the whistles of the railway." He paints a picture of "factories and warehouses approaching as close to the water as they dared, while its wharves and mills and landing stages pulsated with the energies of human life and activities."

This crew of two – George and Clara, generally accompanied by a paid hand – also apparently lived on the boat, an intimate arrangement that eventually produced two more crewmen. Their sons, George and Albert. But they were not destined for life under the brownish-red sails of the Thames sailing barges. As the two boys reached their 20s at the turn of the last century, they were sent away to America. George and Clara sold *Hope* and followed later.

"America was the opportunity," Ernie says. "Anyone that wanted to advance themselves came to America."

They were Ellis Island immigrants. Ernie does not know why the family chose to send the boys on to Rochester, in western New York. He had heard, perhaps in eavesdropping on the conversations of adults when he was a child, that the city at the edge of Lake Ontario was chosen for the unlikely reason that there was a Rochester not far from London. That particular Rochester was, in fact, where many of the Thames sailing barges were constructed. Maybe it was stamped or stenciled on one of the fittings on George and Clara's boat, something they stared at for years while sailing, subliminally planting it in their minds, until the name became familiar. Rochester.

It was a boom town. Like London, Rochester, N.Y., was bisected by a river, with busy industry crowding its shores. Power plants, more than a dozen breweries and mills powered by big wheels that turned in channels, called races, filled with water re-directed from the river. Railroad tracks, including the coach cars of the Buffalo, Rochester & Pittsburgh Railroad, curved gracefully down to the river's edge to meet the *S.S. Ontario No. 1*, a ferry that in five hours could carry 1,000 passengers and rail cars loaded with coal across the lake to the Canadian town 52 miles directly north, Cobourg. Unlike the Thames, however, the Genesee was not crowded with freight-carrying boats, lake steamers and barges, or the pleasure craft of the Rochester Yacht Club. At least, not beyond 2½ miles into the river from where it emptied into the lake. An imposing set of waterfalls saw to that.

George landed a job as a draftsman at Eastman Kodak, the Rochester company whose simplification of the photo process – making it a snap – had taken the camera out of the hands of professionals and turned every family outing into a postcard opportunity. George met another recent

English immigrant, May. They married, and soon had two children themselves: Frank and then, four years later, in 1916, Ernie.

Ernie does not remember his father. With the U.S. plunging into World War I, George never had the opportunity to be a part of what President Woodrow Wilson optimistically called "a war to end all wars." The Influenza Pandemic of 1918 killed an estimated 675,000 Americans, 10 times as many U.S. citizens as would die in the war. Worldwide, perhaps 20 to 40 million died of influenza. George Coleman was among them.

People who know Ernie Coleman always say this of him: He's an average guy. His family circumstances early in his life certainly show as much. The math suggests being 2 years old and fatherless was not an unusual circumstance. The life expectancy of a man born in the late 1880s, as was George Coleman, was 42½ years. He made it to 27. But walk around the cemeteries where they now rest, and by the dates on the graves it becomes quite obvious that George Coleman was pretty average as well. As was his brother, Albert, who died shortly thereafter. Apparently, the culprit was diphtheria. "He was canoeing, and drank the water and died," Ernie says. "That's what I heard."

But the Great Depression, which swept through the world in the fall of 1929 just as swiftly as the Influenza Pandemic had 11 years earlier, was truly the great equalizer.

Decisions were made. Frank stayed with his grandparents. Ernie would live with his mother, who found work with a well-off family as a nanny and housekeeper, moving into an upstairs apartment at their house. And just as Ernie had been too young to be aware of the presence, and then the loss, of his father, he can't remember Alfred Kyle first coming around. Alfred was one of nine brothers and one sister, an ex-Navy man who'd served on the battleship *Iowa* as a fireman, shoveling coal into its boilers. Now he had a job at the Piano Works in East Rochester, forging the cast-iron plates on which the strings were mounted, then burnishing those plates with a polishing rouge to improve the instrument's internal aesthetics. Those pianos quickly left town, spreading music around the world.

Four years after George Coleman died, Alfred married May. With Ernie scurrying about at their feet, the couple moved to an apartment right on the Commercial Street trolley line in downtown East Rochester, Alfred's hometown, before buying a house on Grant Street. Three bedrooms, two stories, a septic tank. The American dream was within reach for them, if it weren't for the economic disaster that was suffocating the world.

"From '29 to '35, it was poverty time," Ernie says. "My mother found 18 different ways to cook hamburger. We had a Victory Garden, my father had chickens on the property. There was a lot of bartering going on. Apparently, we had good production of eggs." Two big trees in the back provided apples to trade for fruit and vegetables. Steaks were for the rich. "Never any meat," Ernie says. "It was too scarce."

As he grew into a teenager and enrolled at East Rochester High School, sports was what mattered. Now the first real picture of Ernie emerges. Competitor. As a tennis player, he had a secret weapon. He was ambidextrous. "I never had a backhand," he says. "I just switched the racket." In baseball, he was a catcher. "I couldn't hit at all, I was terrible," he says. "But I learned to throw to second and I tagged a lot of guys stealing." The school had no hockey team until he and some friends put one together. Although the senior class at East Rochester had only about 75 kids, it was enough to field a football team. Everyone played both offense and defense. It was the leather-helmet era, the forward pass was rarely explored territory. The teams moved on the ground like World War I armies facing each other across No Man's Land. He was a 175-pound center, and on defense took particular pride in rattling the opposite center with chatter about what he was going to do to him. "'OK, I'm gonna climb over you,'" he says. "Next time, 'I'm gonna push you back.' They'd get so nervous, they couldn't pass the ball back."

That's right. Ernie Coleman was a trash talker. But the confident words faded at inopportune times.

"I had an inferiority complex with women," Ernie says. "I worried about what they thought of me." Throughout high school, he had only two dates. And as organizer of the junior prom and senior ball, class of 1935, those dates were mandated. "It was protocol."

The East Rochester High School Glee Club. Ernie is the
handsome lad in the second row, far right.

He hid from that shortcoming among his best friends, The Three
Musketeers. That's what they called themselves. Ernie Coleman, Paul
Smith and Stan Corteville. "We always did everything together," Ernie
says. Sports, swimming in the barge canal. Or downtown Rochester adventures, to "browse around some of the stores and drool," he says. "We
couldn't afford to buy anything." Yet movies at the RKO Palace on North
Clinton and Loews Rochester at Clinton Avenue and Court Street – or-
nate, 3,000-seat theaters with chandeliers and winding staircases – were
within their financial universe. Admission was 15 cents, 25 cents after 6
p.m. "We always got there early," Ernie says. "Absolutely." So absolutely,
you suspect Ernie today would still get to the movies early, if it saved him
a dime. During the Depression, that dime would get him one tiny burger
at the White Castle knockoff of the day, White Tower Hamburgers. If
they were really feeling flush, they'd go to an Italian restaurant on North
Street, Catelli's, and load up on a 20-cent plate of spaghetti. With one
meatball, that's a nickel extra.

It was an era where you entertained yourself. Alfred Kyle not only
made pianos, he played them. The house had an upright piano and he

had a pretty good voice. Ernie and his buddies – "No girls, just guys" – would gather for sing-alongs of the popular music of the day that they heard on the radio. Of course, it was a while before they actually had a radio in the house. Until they could acquire a real one, which in the early 1920s was the financial equivalent of buying a used car, Ernie built a crystal radio. It was a simple device that ran on no outside power, with a long antenna to pick up all available signals, a tuned circuit to select the signal, the crystal detector to process the signal, and earphones to hear it. "You'd pick away, pick away, until you found a station and held it," Ernie says. He and his stepfather listened to the much-anticipated 1927 Jack Dempsey-Gene Tunney heavyweight title fight this way, "the one with the controversy." That was the infamous "Long Count" fight, in which Tunney may have benefited from a few extra seconds after a knockdown, allowing him to recover and win the fight. This was real stepfather-son bonding. Alfred had boxed in the Navy, and evidently brawled his way to the dinner table while growing up. "When you're one of nine boys," Ernie says, "you've got to learn how to handle yourself. He taught me some tricks."

In many ways, this was a romantic vision of American life, but reality was always gnawing at its bones. The reality was, Ernie had to start bringing some money into the household. With the help of a next-door neighbor, an assistant golf pro, Ernie was hired for his first job, caddying at Locust Hill Country Club. Today it is a championship course, the host of LPGA events. But it was less than 10 years old then, carved out of empty farmland in the suburb of Pittsford. Riding his bicycle five miles to the course, he earned 75 cents carrying a set of bags for 18 holes. On Saturdays, he would double up and carry two bags. Maybe not such a big deal, Ernie concedes, as golfers back then carried fewer clubs. As a bonus, some golfers would let the caddies borrow their clubs to play while they held court in the clubhouse. The 75 cents, $1.50 on Saturdays, went into the family fund.

Business setbacks were a constant threat during the Depression, even among the caddies. "The golfers had their favorites," Ernie says. One particular golfer would always ask for Ernie, and "I was happy to know I was doing a good job." But during a tournament elsewhere, the fellow "up and died on the golf course. So I lost him."

Ernie was also walking two miles from school a few times a week to the home of the daughter of the rich family that employed his mother as a nanny. He'd garden, trim trees, mow the lawn. Then he'd walk two miles home with the extra cash, once again, going into the family fund.

That all ended the Monday after the East Rochester class of '35 graduation, when Ernie got his first adult job. No more caddying or mowing. He was now a killer.

Killer of silver foxes, in fact. "The prime ones," Ernie says. It was the Depression, but rich women still loved to drape a shimmering fur around their necks. Catching a car ride each day with the neighbor who had helped him get the job, Ernie was getting $15 a week for six days of work. The farm was home to 500 foxes when he arrived, and Ernie's job at first was pretty simple. "I was the guy that held them when they murdered them," he says. "Strychnine in the heart. One shot, they were dead." He'd flip the body to the skinner, who relieved the animals of their coats in the name of fashion. Then it was Ernie's duty to get rid of the bodies. "It's amazing how small they were without their fur," he says. "They looked like little, tiny greyhounds." He buried them, because "you couldn't use them for dog food, they had strychnine in them."

Despite his self-professed failure at high school romance, Ernie enjoyed better success in the reproductive sciences with foxes. The farm wanted to double the number of animals, and Ernie was assigned to watch the breeding. "There were three pairs we had to be very careful about," he says, "because the males would eat the pups. The minute we saw a fox was pregnant, we had to separate them."

Ernie's role in romancing the stoles must have been a success: The farm was up to about 800 foxes by the time he left that job, taking one with a fireworks factory, east of East Rochester, near where Midvale Golf Course is today. Ernie's job was assembling skyrockets and Roman candles, and he was good at it. For the skyrockets, he had a box with 72 slots in it, one slot for each one of 72 skyrockets. He'd sift the gunpowder into the holes, pack an igniter pellet into each one, then press the lid down tight. Ernie was particularly excited about one final step, testing the fireworks.

His enthusiasm for this aspect of the job took him to new heights in the profession one afternoon.

Each man assembling fireworks worked in his own little shed, for good reason. In the event of an explosion, it wouldn't take down the entire operation. "Everything was brass, I thought," Ernie says of the rig that he used to fashion the fireworks, "so I thought there would be no sparks." But one afternoon, as he tamped down the powder, a spark met Ernie's rack of fireworks. When he realized what was about to happen, he turned and ran, and his co-workers were treated to a surreal scene, he says. "The door blew off and I was riding on it, like a magic carpet, they said. I didn't get hurt. Just tumbled into the grass, a little stunned." Perhaps, he speculates, his ability to deal with the rough landing had something to do with one of The Three Musketeers' Depression-era moneymaking schemes. They'd created a tumbling team, putting on shows at the Rotary Club and at halftime of high-school basketball games. They made up the routines themselves. The tumbling team, Ernie says, "taught me a lot about how to handle myself in the air."

Such seemingly inconsequential experiences, such as the fearlessness that comes with defying gravity, have served Ernie well over the years.

Having survived the fireworks episode, Ernie moved on to another job, at the Merchants Despatch Transportation Co., refurbishing refrigerated railroad cars. They stripped the cars of their timber frames and the wood was set aside for anyone who wanted it. "Of course, it was full of nails," Ernie says. "So you had to pull nails." Much of this abandoned lumber went into building the shambling summer homes perched on the edge of Lake Ontario, in an eight-street community that was called White City then, sometimes referred to as Tent City, after the white canvas of the tents that lined the neighborhood. The area evolved into part of the more resort-sounding Summerville as the homes took on permanent status. Years later, in the '60s, Ernie would buy one of them, the house on Madison Terrace where he could look out the little window and see the lake. He's expanded on the house's basic, 72-foot-long shotgun-shack design, knocking off 40 feet of it and putting a two-story addition on the back. The little patio table at the side of the house, beneath the shade of an impressively tall tulip tree, next to the white hydrangeas, was where he sat in the summer of 2010, a 93-year-old man telling his story.

A couple of years out of high school, and as an ambitious working man, Ernie had acquired his first car by borrowing $25 from his grandmother, "Because my folks didn't have any money." It was a green 1926 Chevy, used, "with bald tires and no side skirts." He gave his grandmother $2.50 a week until the loan was paid off.

An obvious pattern emerges during these Depression days. A constant shuffling from job to job. "The jobs evaporated. You had to," Ernie says. It was the same for his brother, who tried a scheme that involved buying canoes and renting them at Mendon Ponds Park. That didn't work. It was the Depression; people spent their recreation money with restraint, and the quiet of a canoe pond excursion couldn't keep up with the crowds at Lake Ontario Beach and Sea Breeze Amusement Park with the wooden Jack Rabbit roller coaster and huge Danceland ballroom, dominated by a ceiling mirror ball.

One of the canoes ended up as Ernie's high school graduation present, as Frank abandoned wilderness amusements in favor of driving through Monroe County in his Model-T sedan, selling detergent at 10 cents a bottle. Their stepfather wasn't immune to the job shuffle. He was laid off from the Piano Works in 1937, but May would have nothing to do with welfare. Her husband soon took a job, at $9 a week, with the Public Works Administration, Franklin Roosevelt's massive make-work program for the millions of unemployed. Alfred built trails and small buildings in Mendon Ponds Park, until a few years later he was back at the Piano Works, working in the building's power plant. He was back at the bottom, shoveling coal into the building's boilers, just as he had on the *Iowa*, slowly moving up the job ladder until he retired many years later.

But when his car-rehab job evaporated as well, Ernie did take the unemployment. His first check was for $21. "That was big money there, for doing nothing," he says. Decades later, he can still recall these seemingly insignificant figures. Seventy-five cents to carry a golf bag, $15 a week to kill foxes. Or how much he paid for a hamburger, 10 cents. It was the Depression, every dime was important.

Ernie was competitive, but we also see that he was resourceful. The unemployment money gave him the chance to take classes in operating lathing and planing equipment at the college downtown, the grandly named Rochester Athenaeum and Mechanics Institute. It later became Rochester Institute of Technology and by 1968, as was the case with many people and businesses, had fled to the suburbs.

"At that time I had been hounding Gleason Works," Ernie says. Gleason Works, even today, is a long, oddly elegant factory sprawling a couple of blocks along University Avenue. Back then, the company's major function was cutting gears for heavy military armaments. After his short period of unemployment and college courses, Ernie was hired on as a machinist in 1938, working the gear-cutting machinery. Sixty-five cents an hour.

Just as the jobs had been racing through his hands, other aspects of Ernie's life were as well. His mother was ill. Peritonitis, it was at first thought. But really, "They didn't know what it was," Ernie says. "They opened her up, saw what it was, closed her up, that was it. It was just a matter of time." Colon cancer claimed her a few months later.

And, as if making up for lost time, the kid who couldn't talk to girls at East Rochester High School now had a girlfriend. The Three Musketeers had rented a cottage for a week on Canandaigua Lake, and Ernie met Ruth Naramore. They were married in March of 1938 and lived with his parents for a while, until Ernie's brother – now managing a seed company – told him about the second half of the duplex he was living in, on Marion Street, just a few blocks from Gleason Works. Good enough for a newly married couple.

The Depression was fading from the landscape. "I was always optimistic," Ernie says. "I could see it getting better." World War II erupted, and the United States economy was benefiting, manufacturing goods and weapons for a conflict from which it had largely kept its distance, until Dec. 7, 1941. After the Japanese bombed Pearl Harbor, the United States was fully engaged in a world war. But not if you were employed by

Gleason Works. "Anybody in the war effort, making stuff for World War II, was exempt," Ernie says. "You were 4-F."

But just because you were 4-F didn't mean you couldn't read the newspapers, or see the newsreels before the start of the movies. The Japanese had pushed the U.S. forces out of the Philippines. The Germans were massing troops on the coast of France, staring across the English Channel, and driving tanks through the African desert alongside the Italians. Men would be needed. Men, probably, like Frank. Selling seeds wasn't vital to the war effort.

Ernie began to think. His brother was married, with a young child. If he joined the service, maybe they would leave Frank out of the war. It was an interesting scheme, selfless for sure. But, "I didn't tell him that," Ernie says. "I wanted to go anyway. I wasn't getting along too well at home. My wife was a social climber, and I'm not."

So Ernie joined the Navy, and the war. To see the world, and get away from the war on the home front. "We had a lot of conflict," he says of Ruth. "I wanted to get away. Sailing wasn't enough."

Chapter Three

Rochester is no longer the thriving place that it was when George and Frank Coleman arrived from England. It has grown, but like many eastern cities is struggling with the loss of its manufacturing base, the remains of much of it still visible as abandoned buildings and vegetation-covered foundations along the Genesee River. Still, a million people live and work in Monroe County, and the glow from the city's lights obscures the stars at night. When you sail a few miles out into Lake Ontario, many more stars become apparent. The Milky Way emerges as a thin veil of cosmic clutter tracing its way across the sky, the edge of our galaxy.

Ernie has seen the Northern Lights here many times, to the point that he seems a bit bored with the shimmering curtain of greens, blues and whites. "I haven't looked for that in five years," he says. Some long-time sailors, seemingly steady fellows, will tell you they've seen other unexplained lights in the night sky. In his more than 70 years on the lake, Ernie has seen no such thing. He's more interested in the dot of green that sometimes appears on the top edge of the sun, just as it dips below the horizon. It's the refraction of higher-frequency light, green, traveling along the thinner edge of the atmosphere, after the curvature of the earth itself has obstructed the yellows and reds of the sun moving through the lower, denser atmosphere. The prism effect lasts one or two seconds, and it is very tiny.

Lake Ontario is the smallest of the five Great Lakes, but shallower Lake Erie is actually the lesser by volume. Huron, Michigan and Superior are much larger, although sailors will tell you that that the two small, shallow-bottomed lakes are more easily riled when difficult weather rolls in. Ernie has seen waterspouts, the tornado-like funnel clouds over the lake, he says, "from a distance." Although they are much weaker than tornadoes over land, reports of waterspouts damaging boats do exist, particularly boats tied to their piers. So from a distance is the safe way to watch them.

Sailors must be mindful of other dangers. High in the mast, most sailboats wear a radar reflector, a volleyball-sized octrahedral presenting several reflecting surfaces, a better target for a large ship's radar. Big freighters and tankers share the water with pleasure boats, and while accidents are rare, they happen. In 2006, off England's Isle of Wight, a yacht named *Ouzo* and its crew of three were lost when it either collided with a large ferry or perhaps was swamped by the ferry's wake. Ernie's been as close as 75 yards to a big lake freighter. "Scary," he says. "Those suckers can't stop. You see that thing coming up, with the bow wave swinging along."

For many long minutes after spotting a ship on the horizon, a sailboat can't be certain where the bigger vessel is heading. "Finally, I realized if you see both sides of a ship" – the bow and the stern – "you're safe," Ernie says. "If you see only one side...." That's not good. It's coming toward you.

But the most common danger is the unexpected storm. He's sailed through some big ones, of course, and even seen the static electricity that can envelop a boat. They call it St. Elmo's Fire, "running and dancing up and down the rigging," Ernie says. He describes it as whitish-blue, and it only lasts four to five seconds. "Its very bad for the instruments," Ernie says, recalling a race where four boats lost their speed indicators, radios and depth sounders, "the whole works, just wiped it all out." He once saw the antenna for own his LORAN, the radio-navigation system, "start humming like a bumblebee. A big bumblebee." Ernie yelled for one of his crew to quickly turn it off, saving the equipment. Sailing is a sport, a recreation, a relaxing afternoon, but many times arise when you have to think quickly.

It is long past time to slow down. Ernie has been racing 72 years. He has been through a handful of boats, but since 1975 he's settled in with *Desire*, a Columbia 26. The name came to him in a dream. At 26 feet long, *Desire* is big enough to handle the 52-mile crossing to Canada. It is a cruising boat, not a racer, but "the boat doesn't know that," Ernie says.

"I've seen strong winds, lots of rain. I've been in 40-mile winds in that boat." *Desire* is often not the fastest boat in the race. But that's OK, because boats are assigned handicaps in the world of lake racing. This isn't the America's Cup, where the multi-millionaire with the latest equipment wins. These races are a test of the sailors, not the boats. And to the slowest can come the spoils. Ernie recalls a day where he and another Columbia 26 were rated the weakest boats in the race. The two boats eased along, trailing far behind the rest of the pack. The hares had all crossed the finish line when the wind suddenly picked up – blowing a real stink, in sailor language – and scooted the two Columbia 26s along quickly enough that, with their handicaps factored in, resulted in a one-two finish for the tortoises. Slow and steady can indeed win the race.

It is Ernie's life philosophy as well. At 93, he still drives a car, and is amused by other drivers who display impatience at intersections. "What's the hurry?" he asks. "Where are you going? What time are you going to save, two minutes? I think that has had a lot to do with my success in racing. Take your time, look around. Look where the other guy is. Get to know the speed of your boat. It's all experience. I've been racing for 71 years, and I can't recall two races that were the same."

Typical of such atypical sails was a Rochester Yacht Club annual Fourth of July cruise across the lake in the mid-1990s, to Cobourg, Canada. "The wind was out of the west, very strong," Ernie says. It started with three-foot waves, and then a storm warning: All small boats take refuge. *Desire*, with Ernie and Marilyn aboard, was far beyond the midpoint of Lake Ontario by then. "Am I supposed to put the thing on my shoulder and go home?" Ernie laughs.

Sure, he laughs now. They were sailing the trough then between eight-foot waves. "I told Marilyn, 'Don't look back,' " Ernie says. She would have seen that the waves were higher than the boat. He was calculating what arrangement of sails would slow *Desire*, which sail he could let out while still retaining enough speed that he could steer the boat, rather than allow the lake do with it what it will. And he was calculating how to limit damage to the boat, if it came to that. Which sail he would prefer to sacrifice. "I let the main out, spilled some wind," Ernie says.

"What cost more, the main or the jib? I let the jib out. The boat was shaking like a leaf. I was afraid the boat would shake apart."

They were the last ones to arrive in port. *Desire* was still under full sail a mere 200 feet from the Cobourg harbor entrance before Ernie dared take down the sails and limp in to the dock on his motor. It was a dramatic arrival, and the other sailors hooted in mock approval. "Little did they know," Ernie says of *Desire*'s charge into the harbor, "I couldn't do anything about it."

It wasn't classic textbook sailing, but Ernie has never had a formal class. He sails on instinct. "It just came naturally," he says. "I guess I inherited it from my grandfather. Incidentally, I'm still learning."

Mastering sailing techniques can fill a lifetime. It starts with the sails and the tell-tale, a strip of fabric attached to the aft edge of the mainsail, the largest sail on the boat. If the tell-tale is streaming backward, you're fine. The jib, the triangular sail set at the front of the mast, is generally outfitted with tell-tales as well. If any of the tell-tales begin spinning and fluttering, it's telling the sailor that the wind isn't hitting the sails properly, and the boat must be edged over a bit in that direction. "Sail trim is the motor of the boat," Ernie says. "The better you trim it, the faster you go."

The wind was once the only way to move a boat such distances. Sails were a necessity. Not anymore. But still, the moment the motor goes off, the sails go up, and the silence it brings is what draws sailors like Ernie out onto the lake. "It was the thrill of being on water, under motion with no noise," he says. "I loved it. I still love it. We'd go out, and I couldn't wait to get the motor turned off."

The motor. That's the enemy. Most sailboat owners are dismissive of powerboats. They call them "stinkpots."

Destination rarely matters. Unlike the landscape, which quickly becomes a fading line of dull green off the stern, the seascape shifts with each voyage onto the lake. The water surface changes. The wind changes. He and Marilyn will return from a sail and friends would say, " 'Where'd you go?' " Ernie says. " 'Back and forth, four or five miles.' We can really relax out there."

Out there a sailor can hear the cry of sea birds, or the wind catching the sail, the slap of water against the hull, or the metallic tap, tap, tap of the lines against the aluminum mast. But mostly, silence. This is a time for thinking. Or not thinking.

"Nothing," Ernie says of what passes through his mind at such moments. "Just plain enjoying. I'm always watching the sail, to trim it. It's just my nature."

Also in his nature: "If there's another boat out there, he's racing," Ernie says. "Whether he knows it or not."

Chapter Four

As 1933 drew to a close, the Bethlehem Shipping Company's Fore River plant at Quincy, Mass., was preparing to begin work on the last of the seven ships that would later be named the *New Orleans* class of heavy cruisers. This one would be *USS Vincennes*. The keel was laid on Jan. 2, 1934, and, over the next three years, would grow to 588 feet long, 61 feet and 10 inches wide, its eight boilers and four propellers capable of moving it along at about 32 knots. Miss Harriet Virginia Kimmell, daughter of the mayor of Vincennes, Ind., was brought east to preside over the launching ceremony of the still-incomplete shell.

The war machine that she christened, amid the flags and bunting and social events that surrounded the occasion, would soon be fitted with a main battery of nine eight-inch guns mounted in three triple turrets, each gun capable of firing a 355-pound shell 31,700 yards, piercing five inches of armor plate. A crew of 952 officers and enlisted men would tend to the needs of this ship. With Europe still piled high with the ruins of World War I, and memories aching from the devastation that explosives and steel could do to servicemen and civilians alike, this class of warship was designed within the limitations of the Washington Naval Treaty of 1921, and later the London Naval Treaty. The United States Navy intended it to be matched up against one potential opponent in particular: A ship of the same heavy cruiser category, manned by a Japanese crew.

As *Vincennes* was emerging from the drawing board in 1933, so was 16-year-old Ernie's first boat, in the garage of his family's home in East Rochester. He had closely examined photos of sailboats, assembling a tiny paper prototype, "and that proved successful," he says. Why wouldn't a scaled-up version work as well? "I had help from my stepfather," Ernie says. "He was a pretty good carpenter, although he never pursued it as a trade." Ernie himself cut out the rudder in shop class. The finished boat was 12 feet long, four feet wide, flat-bottomed with slightly curving sides. "And heavy, quite heavy," Ernie says.

Boatbuilding, he admits, was something "I learned all by my lonesome." Perhaps a little bit of a knowledgeable crowd would have been in order. When it was completed, he and fellow Musketeer Paul Smith hauled the boat to nearby Canandaigua Lake, launched it, and sailed downwind about a mile before deciding to turn back.

Lacking a proper keel, the boat was simply pushed sideways by any wind gusting in from the side. The two boys crippled the boat back to the beach and walked it home, like a dog on a leash. "I gave it to a neighbor," Ernie says. "He turned it into a fishing boat."

So his first attempt to answer the call of the wind and waves had come to an ignominious end, a pile of lumber in the shape of a boat now sentenced to plodding through the rocks and algae of the lakeshore, searching for brown trout. Ernie never even had the opportunity to give his first attempt at boatbuilding a proper name. "I gave it a lot of names because it wouldn't sail," Ernie concedes. "But that was different."

That wouldn't be the end of his sailing ambitions. The DNA wouldn't allow it.

Yet perhaps Ernie would not have moved beyond the casual interest of any kid building model sailboats out of balsa wood, and then past the failure of his first boat, were it not for his family having built a cottage at Canandaigua Lake, and the prodding from the constant presence of those sailboats skipping along the waves. At 11½ miles long and 1½ miles wide, Canandaigua is the fourth-largest of the Finger Lakes, long traces of fresh water spread out like the fingers of a pair of giant hands resting on the rural landscape of western New York. Lakes created by a series of glacial movements beginning two million years ago in the Pleistocene Era, ice sheets more than two miles deep descending from Hudson Bay.

About 11,000 years after the last of these glaciers had retreated deep into Canada, in 1932, Ernie's parents paid $100 for a lot at Crystal Beach, about seven miles down the east side of Canandaigua Lake. Working on weekends, Ernie, Frank and their stepfather finished the cottage in one summer.

Now Ernie was tantalizingly close to the water. Sailboats were scooting up and down the lake all around him. He wanted to join them. Sailing had skipped a generation in the Coleman family, bounding from George to Ernie over his two fathers. Ernie's biological father may have grown up on a Thames sailing barge, but he had chosen the stability of a drafting board before his life was cut short. Ernie's stepfather actually did have a boat, but to Ernie that one didn't measure up. It was a small boat with a motor, for fishing only. "He was an enthusiastic fisherman," Ernie says, without showing any enthusiasm for the subject himself; remember, he considered his first boatbuilding project to be a failure after it ended up as a mere carp trawler. And he has never had any interest in fish, unless it's dinnertime. To Ernie, the water has never been about what lies beneath.

His flat-bottomed, keel-less disaster had been the first attempt. Ernie had to wait nearly two years before the next opportunity presented itself. It came with his graduation from high school, when he unexpectedly had a boat on his hands: The canoe his brother had given him as a graduation present.

It was the wrong kind of craft, as far as Ernie was concerned, and in rough shape. But just as he had learned the principles of carpentry while helping build the family summer cottage, the cottage project had also sharpened his resourcefulness. To get the materials to build the cottage, the family had borrowed the milkman's truck to move lumber from where many people in East Rochester were getting it during the Great Depression, rummaging through the rough piles ripped from the rail cars being rebuilt at the Merchants Despatch Transportation Co.

Ernie's second sailboat would be the product of a similar resourcefulness. He fit a 10-foot mast with a boom to the bottom of the canoe, with a sail made from an old bed sheet. Maybe a little top-heavy but, "I was the ballast," Ernie says. He steered it with a paddle. If the wind died away completely, he'd use the paddle to get back home. A neighbor gave him a leeboard – a plank that fits on the side of the boat, enabling it to sail into the wind a bit, something lacking in the first home-built craft that he had been forced to walk home on its maiden voyage. Leeboards are not unknown in American sailing waters, but they're not particularly common, either. But they were quite frequently seen on Thames sailing barges.

And this boat worked. "I used to sail that thing all over the place," Ernie says. But it was just a first successful step. A neighbor had a 14-foot dinghy stored in a shed, an International 14, often called a cat boat, and suggested Ernie buy it from him. The asking price was $75. Ernie didn't have that kind of money, but the neighbor turned it over to him anyway. "He said give me $5 whenever you can find it," Ernie says. After about $25 in payments, the neighbor called it a done deal.

As dinghies go, this one was a bit dinged up. "It leaked like a sieve, it was so dry," Ernie says. The boat was of lapstrake construction, with successive, overlapping curved planks built up from the keel, and a mast set at the forward end. Enlisting the help of the seemingly always available Smitty – the third Musketeer, Corteville, had been enjoying success with girls that had escaped the other two – Ernie set about the tedious task of re-riveting the entire boat and pouring varnish into the cracks.

The rehab was a success. It sailed, and well. But the boat wasn't quite the right fit. The competitor in Ernie wanted to race those other guys chasing the Canandaigua Lake winds. And there, he had the wind taken from his sails. Boats race against each other in categories, established by governing bodies in much the same way that the capabilities of the warships of the time were governed by naval treaties. Each sailboat category bears specific limitations on measurable aspects such as size, weight and sails. Ernie's boat was too old; the local sporting world had passed it by. No one was racing International 14s around western New York anymore.

And too, there was the matter of the cottage that The Three Musketeers had rented in the summer of 1937, the high-school sorority that had moved into the cabin next door, and the nearby dance hall. He was finished with high school, but Ernie was suddenly doing quite well in chemistry. His girlfriend, Ruth, was occupying more of his time. "Things went off pretty well, all of a sudden, Pow! The fact I was so self-conscious in high school," he says, his voice trailing off.... "The fact that a girl paid so much attention to me, I was taken over."

Meanwhile, on Irondequoit Bay, a natural harbor formed by Lake Ontario pushing its way into the shoreline, the boat that everyone was racing was a new design. A simple, 15½-foot, two-man dinghy called the Snipe. Three of them had come in from California and dominated some of the local races. By 1936, just five years after it had been designed and the first one built, the Snipe had become the most popular racing class in the world.

Ernie had been romancing Ruth with boat rides – a whirlpool romance that would too quickly lead to marriage less than a year later. It wasn't much after that, Ernie says, that he'd discovered three things. One, Ruth liked to talk. Two, she really wasn't much interested in sailing. And three, he had to have one of those new boats to get into the racing scene.

Ernie's solution – his solution to two of those three problems, anyway – was to buy a Snipe kit. Once again he went to work in the garage of the Grant Street house, where he had a little room to spread out the boat parts, and room for himself. "It didn't amount to much," he recalls. "Just a frame."

And, he confesses, "It was kind of an out for me, to get away from Ruth."

With the completion of the Snipe, which he named *Kiddo,* Ernie was now on equal footing with his new sailing friends at the bay's Newport Yacht Club. Better footing, actually, as the races unfolded. While Ruth was ashore, socializing with the other wives and girlfriends, the inexperienced Ernie was actually winning. He was collecting trophies, his success preventing him from incorporating the mistakes of others into his own sailing style. "I knew nothing about racing," he says. "I was so far ahead, I never learned there's rules of the road." The old road, it turns out, was the wrong direction. Ernie's boat was faster because it was lighter. Rather than tying his boat to the pier after the race, he'd built himself a haul-out, cranking *Kiddo* out of the water to dry after each outing. "All of their boats soaked up water and had growth on them," Ernie says. "Here I come down with a free boat. Well, they were no match for me."

Soon, his competitors wanted growth-free boats, and they were willing to pay for it. "Before the summer was out," Ernie says, "I built a haul-out for every boat."

But that wasn't the only secret. He'd outfitted the Snipe with a daggerboard, more commonly called a centerboard these days, a blade-like retractable keel that gives a small sailboat more stability and enables it to make its way upwind more easily. That's not a new invention. In 2008, a couple of shipwreck hunters found a 55-foot schooner, equipped with a daggerboard, on the bottom of Lake Ontario, 10 miles off the southern coast. Ernie and thousands of other sailors had probably passed peacefully over that piece of history many times since it sank in the early 1800s.

After the other Newport Yacht Club sailors picked up on Ernie's daggerboard, many of them wanted one as well. Ernie traced out a pattern, took it to a salvage yard, and had a handful of them cut from scrap steel. By then, he and Ruth were living in the Marion Street duplex with Frank and his wife and their young son. Ernie would bring the roughed-out daggerboards home, take them down to the basement and grind the edges down with equipment he'd borrowed from Gleason Works.

He also had an old box of fireworks stored beneath the basement steps from his days at the fireworks factory. Maybe 100 pieces of colorful explosives. He and his brother were grinding away at a daggerboard when a shower of sparks landed in the box. "I dove into the coal bin," Ernie says. "He went under a table." The box went off in a series of percussive echoes. Ruth was not amused. "I didn't make any brownie points that day," Ernie says. "The whole house smelled of fireworks."

That was a Saturday evening. The next afternoon, Ernie and Frank had moved the grinding operation out to the backyard. "It was a nice day," Ernie recalls. A December Sunday. Frank's wife was inside the house at Marion Street. The radio was on. "She hollered out," as Ernie remembers it, " 'The Japanese are bombing Pearl Harbor!' "

Chapter Five

That December morning, *Vincennes* was already at war, with Hitler and nature. During the year, the ship had been engaged in a series of training exercises and neutrality patrols in the Caribbean Sea and the North Atlantic Ocean, undeclared battlegrounds where German U-boats were stalking cargo ships heavily laden with Franklin D. Roosevelt's "Arsenal of Democracy." The lifeline of weapons and supplies served as an intravenous line directly into England, which was now virtually alone aftet the fall of France. Those cargoes very likely included armored vehicles, aircraft and cannon whose inner workings featured the precision gears that Ernie had helped manufacture at Gleason Works.

American neutrality knew no boundaries. As the Japanese planes appeared over the Pearl Harbor morning sky, it was already the early evening off the coast of South Africa, where *Vincennes* was a part of the U.S. Navy escort for Convoy WS-12X, American transports carrying British troops. The ships were fighting through a fierce gale, with nearly every cruiser and destroyer sustaining some damage. On *Vincennes*, a motor whaleboat was smashed and a Curtiss SOC Seagull floatplane was torn from the deck, the waves slapping it against the catapult silos and hangar doors, like a cat with a yarn toy, before it was swept over the side. This was rough enough, until word began to arrive of what had happened on the other side of the world at Pearl Harbor.

For most Americans, the war had been a distant transmission, something filed by foreign correspondents for newspapers and magazines, or on radio and TV and the Pathé Newsreels of the day, shown in movie theaters before the start of the main feature. This was a big year for movies, with *Citizen Kane, The Maltese Falcon, Dumbo* and Alfred Hitchcock's

Suspicion all on screens in 1941. The effect on military recruiting leveled by one of the most popular films of the year, Bud Abbott and Lou Costello's *Buck Privates*, is open for debate.

"There was a war and we were concerned about the Allies," Ernie says. "We kept track of it. Hitler did a number on Europe, and the bombing of London. We were squeezing for the Allies to stop him. The assassination of the Jews, that was horrible. Now they're trying to say that didn't happen...."

The Holocaust was indeed happening, Hitler was invading the Soviet Union, and Ernie suspected that the United States would be drawn into the European war. But he was shocked when the first move was made by Japan.

"Oh yes, absolutely," he says. "They really took us by total surprise. If they followed up, they could have captured the Hawaiian Islands. We didn't have much of a force there."

Gleason Works, Ruth and now the Imperial Japanese Navy were too much for one man to handle: Ernie signed on in the spring of 1942. "I called my draft board and told them I wanted to volunteer with the Navy," he says. "I joined the Navy, naturally, because I'm a sailor." As for Ruth, "She wasn't happy about it," Ernie says. "I wanted to do my effort, to be a good American citizen. I also wanted to seek some adventure."

His first muster ordinarily would have not have been far at all, Sampson Naval Base on Seneca Lake. However, Ernie recalls it as being under a scarlet fever quarantine at the time. Instead, he was ordered to the Great Lakes Naval Training Station, and a train ride to the huge, self-supporting facility on the west shore of Lake Michigan, north of Chicago. A thousand miles from the closest ocean. Before Pearl Harbor, it had been supporting 10,000 Navy men. In the year after the attack, the training station exploded to handling 75,000 recruits, most bound for the Pacific.

"I didn't know what was in store for me," Ernie says. If he had been paying attention during *Buck Privates*, he would have known it was boot camp, starting with calisthenics at 6 a.m., then classes in aircraft recognition and Naval regulations. "No gun training, they just explained it all," Ernie says. "All of the firearms were in service."

Most importantly, "There's a right way and the Navy way," they were told. "You do it the Navy way."

They learned the Navy way for three weeks. A little shorter than the usual stint – but bodies were needed – followed by a week furlough at home. Back in Rochester, Ernie was nothing special as he walked around in his uniform. A lot of the guys were doing it. They would soon find themselves being sent to exotic-sounding places like Bataan, Morocco and the Aleutian Islands. And Rochester? "Everyone said, 'It's a good place to be from,' " Ernie says. " 'A *long* way from.' "

They got their wish soon enough. "Off to war," Ernie says. Three days on a train across America. "We spent most of it on sidings, I think," he says, until the last stop: Pleasanton, Calif. Sixty miles east of San Francisco. This was the newly activated Camp Shoemaker, a vast tract of wood barracks that was a part of the Navy's rapidly evolving Fleet City, three landlocked bases lying side by side by side that served as the gateway to the war for many sailors.

Here, Ernie ran headlong into the classic military oxymoron of Hurry Up and Wait. "You muster in at 8 a.m.," he says. "If your name wasn't on the list, you had until the next morning." For Ernie, this went on for weeks, plenty of time for the average sailor to get himself embroiled in a handful of episodes not addressed in *The Bluejacket's Manual.* Ernie – who was 25 years old, older than a lot of these kids waiting for their assignments – had a curiosity that ran a little deeper than the USO dances. "I was very interested in history. I wasn't a typical sailor, find the first bar," Ernie says. He took the trains and buses to San Jose and Berkeley, "just to see different areas." He stopped at museums, took in the scenery, wandered out to the wharf and San Francisco's fishing village, inspected an old sailing ship tied to the pier. He rode the trolley to the beach, "loaded with sea gulls and seals," Ernie says. "They had a museum showing the fish that were caught off the pier that was there, various artifacts that were a part of San Francisco."

He was a tourist, but trouble did find him. Late one night in San Francisco, "I was alone waiting to catch a bus," Ernie says, when he was confronted by three zoot suiters. Young guys in outrageous long coats with oversized shoulders, long key chains, pork-pie hats and baggy, peg-legged trousers. The sailors had been warned about these guys. "They were against the war," Ernie says. "They attacked me on a corner."

Fortunately, it was a construction site, with lumber lying about, and the future carpenter knew a few uses for a 2x4 besides wall studs. He picked up a board and began nailing one of the zoot suiters. "Needless to say, they backed off, yelling obscenities," Ernie says.

He had unwittingly been caught up in a battle of cultures, originating on the West Coast in the 1930s in racial tension between whites and Mexican immigrants. The whites accused the Latinos of taking jobs from them, a battle cry that is familiar even into the 21st century. By wartime, the confrontation was frequently seen as a patriotic one by the whites, who interpreted the flamboyant zoot suits as a deliberate flouting of war rationing; wool was one of the early items to be rationed by the War Production Board, resulting in conservatively cut fashions. By 1943, the zoot suit culture had expanded to include both blacks and Mexican-Americans, frequently scuffling with the predominantly white sailors of the West Coast. This bad alchemy exploded in Los Angeles on a series of nights when gangs of sailors and civilians marched down the streets, beating up any zoot suiters they could get their hands on, often tearing off their zoot suits and burning them in the streets. Some people saw these avenging sailors as patriots cleaning up the streets of Los Angeles. But the true nature of the movement was clear, with a committee established to study the riots immediately after the fighting had ended determining that the conflict had been fueled by racism.

Yet, in telling the story all of these years later, Ernie makes no mention of the zoot suiters' race. If it had mattered at all to him back then, their race was no longer worth mentioning for this 93-year-old sailor. They were just weirdly outfitted guys "against the war."

One morning at 8 a.m., shortly after his brush with the zoot suiters, Ernie's name was on the Camp Shoemaker assignment sheet. He was dispatched to Treasure Island, in the midst of San Francisco Bay, to catch an Army transport ship to Hawaii. The next five days were spent cramped alongside fellow servicemen. And to occupy their time? "Nothing," Ernie says. "You're just a passenger. It was a rough ride, a lot of guys got real seasick. I mean, bad, bad." He does not remember the name of the ship. But Ernie says he did hear later that it was torpedoed and sunk somewhere off of Australia.

Carpenter's Mate 2nd Class Ernie Coleman.

In Hawaii came a few more days of waiting, "so I got to see Honolulu for a couple of days," Ernie says. He was a tourist once again, sometimes heading into the city with his alphabet buddy, a Navy postmaster named Richard Bennett. "Everyone went by their last name in the Navy," Ernie says. "Everything was run by the alphabet. He was 'B,' I was 'C.' " Ernie recalls touring the Aloha Tower with its spectacularly huge German-built clock, weighing seven tons, one of the largest clocks in the United States or any of its territories. A grand hotel was nearby. "The boys would come back from a submarine strike, and they'd turn the hotel over to them," Ernie says. "Boy, what they'd do to that hotel, you wouldn't believe. But those boys were under pressure."

Yes, it was sometimes better to forget this was war. The reminder would be posted on the barracks wall at 8 a.m. the next morning: "A... B... C... Coleman, Ernest." He finally had his ship. A heavy cruiser, *USS Vincennes.*

Six months after the Japanese attack, salvage operations at Pearl Harbor had been startlingly effective. As a bus filled with 30 new sailors, including Ernie, followed the road into Pearl, the wrecked aircraft had been swept away, five battleships and two cruisers had been pulled from the harbor mud. However, the capsized *Oklahoma* was still lying like a turtle in Battleship Row. Likewise, the bombed and burned-out battleship *Arizona* was where the Japanese planes had left it, the same place where it sits today as a national monument. It was estimated that 1,500 sailors' bodies were still in those two ships then. Many are still in *Arizona* to this day.

By the time Ernie arrived, *Arizona*'s collapsed forward mast and bridge would have been cut away. But still in place were the mainmast, the stern – slightly broaching the waves – and the ship's big guns, each 50 feet long; in its 26-year history, they had never been fired in wartime, unlike those of the ship on which Ernie was aboard, now leaving the harbor. *Arizona* was already a symbol of another nation's treachery as the United States went to war, just as a half-century earlier another destroyed American battleship, *Maine,* had become a symbol for the country as it charged into the Spanish-American War. (Never mind that the evidence seems clear that the Spanish had nothing to do with that explosion, it's the newspaper headlines that count.)

Today, Ernie shakes his head no when asked if he saw any of this blackened Pearl Harbor wreckage, including this ship that had been the star attraction in the Pathé Newsreels, with photos of its burning wreckage featured prominently in recruiting stations across the country as well. Perhaps *Vincennes* didn't pass close enough, perhaps Ernie was on the wrong side of the ship, or was below decks. Perhaps he didn't wish to see it, or has forgotten it, or has wanted to forget it. If the remains of that terrible December morning were still visible as *Vincennes* left the harbor, for Ernie it's disappeared into that black hole where we put pain. "The barracks were way out of the way," he says. "Honolulu itself is a long way from Pearl Harbor. I was too busy getting acquainted with the ship, finding where my berth was."

In photos, *Vincennes* appears to be quite a pretty ship, if you disregard the deadly intent of its design. Perhaps its lines were a little too busy-looking just aft of amidships, with its two scout seaplanes and their cranes and catapults. *Vincennes* wasn't muscular-looking like so many warships, but lean like a greyhound. And it had a war record. First dodging German U-boats in the Atlantic and Caribbean, then transferring to the Pacific in time to participate in one of the most ambitious schemes of the early months of the war, helping escort the aircraft carrier *Hornet* to within bomber range of Japan. From there, on the morning of April 16, 1942, still 650 miles from their target, Jimmy Doolittle's 16 B-25 bombers left *Hornet* and dropped a handful of bombs on the island nation. Little damage was done, but the U.S. had demonstrated that Japan was not safely beyond the range of the war.

After that mission, the busy *Vincennes* arrived too late to participate in the Battle of Coral Sea in early May, but it was a part of the most important naval action of the Pacific war. On June 4, at the Battle of Midway, American carrier-based planes sank four Japanese carriers. *Vincennes* was assigned to the force protecting the American carriers, its anti-aircraft batteries shooting down one Japanese dive bomber.

In early July, *Vincennes* was once more war bound, although Ernie's duties as it left Hawaii would hardly be any threat to the Japanese. He was "chipping paint, stripping the deck, chipping more paint. It was a steel hull, the salt water rusted it pretty bad." They were touching up the

Measure 12 camouflage scheme, with drooping light and dark shades of gray, and broad red stripes across the top of each gun turret so the ship could be identified by American pilots as one of their own. But being topside chipping paint was better than duty below in the firerooms, the ship's boilers where the temperature could reach 140 degrees.

Ernie had successfully applied for a position as carpenter's mate. To the Navy, that meant more studying, more tests. "How to hold a hammer," Ernie says, that sort of thing. "There was always a carpenter's shop on a ship, and I enjoyed doing it." The Navy was his vocational school, like the Rochester Athenaeum and Mechanics Institute without the eight-inch guns. Ernie was calculating where this might lead. "I might get to be a carpenter and get paid for it," he says. "Wages were very good for the carpenters."

As could be demonstrated by a storm like the one that *Vincennes* had weathered off the coast of South Africa on Dec. 7, even steel ships need carpenters. Cabinets must be repaired, and similar trim set in order. For this, *Vincennes'* carpenter shop was outfitted just like any shop: "Band saw, table saw, a planer," Ernie says. "I don't know why a planer, maybe hobby lobby for some officer." Hobby lobby is a phrase Ernie uses frequently. It's carpentry for fun.

A ship's carpenter has combat assignments as well. "He's a guy that plugs up the holes when it gets blasted," Ernie says. This was done with mattresses and 2x4s. "What else could you do?" Ernie asks. "In a hurry like that? Stuff a mattress, brace it with a pole and hope it works." The poles, with a board nailed across one end in a T shape, were 2x4s bracketed together so that the length of the pole could quickly be adjusted to fit the situation, and keep the mattress nice and tight against unplanned structural events, like a torpedo hole in the hull. Ernie would use poles rigged just like that years later on the job as a civilian carpenter.

Odd as it sounds, a mattress is an old solution to an even older problem: how to plug a hole in a ship's hull. A mattress shoved into the opening after a collision with another ship failed to keep the passenger steamer *Lady Elgin* from sinking in Lake Michigan in 1860, with a huge loss of life. But the practice continued into World War II, with mattresses used to fill holes in the waterline of the carrier *Enterprise* after it was hit by torpedoes in August 1942 at the Battle of the Eastern Solomons. During the Battle of Leyte Gulf in 1944, the *Claxton* used mattresses to shore up the 9 x 5 foot hole left on the waterline after the destroyer was struck by a kamikaze plane. Both ships survived.

Mattresses were the Navy way. In *The Bluejacket's Manual*, the crews on damaged ships are advised to use mattresses or kapok-filled life preservers to stanch the flow of water in the midst of battle:

"In an emergency repair situation, do your best with what you have. If you are calm, alert, and work quickly with the tools you have, you can do much to keep the ship afloat and make her ready for action again."

And in case this hadn't occurred to anyone unfamiliar with the physics of water displacement, *The Bluejacket's Manual* also advises:

"If flooding is not controlled, the ship will sink."

None of this would be of any value to *Vincennes* in the days ahead. In his search for adventure, and whatever it was that he needed to get away from, Ernie was heading toward previously unheard-of destinations on the map: the Solomon Islands, Guadalcanal and New Georgia Sound. There, off Savo Island, he would be a part of one of the most disastrous battles in U.S. Navy history. Ernie does not talk about it. He cannot, even nearly 70 years later.

On Father's Day of 2010, Ernie's family gave him a black, leather-bound journal, urging him to record the memories he had of his 93 years. Dates and friends' names came back to him, a flood of detail that included the jobs he'd held, his four marriages, the boats he'd built, trips to Europe, falling through the ice in a canal. Of *Vincennes*, he only writes:

"Spent time in the Pacific WW2.

"Lost a ship, ended in Maui Hawaii."

Chapter Six

Ernie brings out a handful of photos and spreads them out on the kitchen table. Here's a yellowed image of Ernie and a few teenage pals, including the Musketeer Paul Smith. It was The Great Depression, and they'd driven up to the East Coast after a hurricane had passed through, figuring on getting work with a landscaper. Lots of cleanup to be done. But the jobs didn't materialize, so here they were, laughing, relaxing on a New Jersey beach.

Here is a similarly yellowed image of Ernie, Frank and their mother. They're young men in their 20s. She looks young too, but the cancer that will kill her is probably already spreading though her body.

Here's a fading color picture that looks to be from the late 1960s. It's Ernie's third wife, Evie, wearing some kind of creepy mask, sitting with a neighbor. "He's long gone," Ernie says, a comment that accompanies most of the people in his old photographs. Ernie's also in the photo, although you have to take his word for it. It's Halloween, and he's wearing a costume. "I'd always wanted to be a gorilla," he says. "I jumped up on the bar at the Rochester Yacht Club, making a fool of myself, but the kids loved it." Then he and Evie walked through their neighborhood, trick-or-treating for cocktails.

Here's a recent shot of Ernie's brother, Frank, on the sidewalk outside of the apartment building where he lives in Florida, learning to use a walker. He'd started falling recently, and his son had insisted. "I don't want to use a walker," Frank had grumped. "It makes me look old." He is 98.

And here's a photo of *Desire*, tied to a dock, 85 small pennants hanging from all available lines. The poor boat looks like a flapper girl decked out in gold lamé. These were first-place flags won at races and regattas over the years. "I only keep the gold ones," Ernie says.

Chasing the wind has been the consuming passion for this fellow with the oft-repeated mantra of "sailing is my life." The front room of his house, the remaining original 32 feet of shotgun shack that survived his remodeling, is nautical in nature. The narrowness of it, the wood ceiling beams, and the small windows suitable for rolling out muzzle-loading cannon, have the feel of a space on one of Admiral Horatio Nelson's ships of the line. Although Nelson's ships wouldn't have likely had the cozy fireplace at the aft end, with pieces of slate on the floor apron cut and set in place by Ernie himself. The room opens into a kitchen and eating area as the updated aspects of the house begin to take over, accented with rustic little signs proclaiming "I'd Rather Be Sailing" and photos of *Desire*. Some of the family is gathered beneath magnets on the refrigerator door, the rest of them have been relegated to the walls alongside the stairs ascending to the second floor.

The newer section of the house – a family room that's now the first-floor bedroom, spare room, stairs to the second floor – is where the true Ernie sailing shrine begins. Hallway shelves, end tables and the broad top of the big television lined with hardware that is the testimonial to his skills. Silver bowls, brass sailboats, chrome balls, plaques, engraved beer mugs, plastic triangles representing mainsails, all from races of different lengths, on different bodies of water, sponsored by organizations such as the Oak Orchard Yacht Club, 33 miles up the east coast of Lake Ontario. Even awards for winning single-handed races. Ernie has *Desire* rigged so he can handle everything from the cockpit.

He has one trophy that he didn't win. Ernie's youngest daughter, Julie, left it for him. "I took her out for a half hour so she could learn to sail," he says. And the next day she won a race.

"I hope I don't win any more, I've got to clean 'em," Ernie adds, as he carefully makes his way back to the kitchen. After 93 years, he's collected some hardware in his joints as well.

But of course, the pursuit of the perfect sail will continue. Here's the latest trophy, sitting on the kitchen table: Small and rectangular, for a third-place finish two days earlier. "There are two boats out there I absolutely can't beat," he complains. "I'm sure their ratings are wrong." They're Pearson 26s, naturally faster boats than his Columbia, which is a heavy three tons for 26 feet. The lighter Pearsons finished one and two. "They gave us time," Ernie says of the allowances that are supposed to ensure these races are battles of sailors, not technology. "But not enough." Another much longer race had been run the next day, the Hospice Regatta, but "I chose not to go this year, because of the wind and the waves," he says. "When I saw the water, I called the crew up, and they all thanked me. With a boat of my size, it's really tough on a crew to battle waves, high waves, a long distance, when the wind is blowing as strong as it is.

"I race for the enjoyment of being out there. When there's harsh conditions, I don't see any need for competing. I'm not that gung-ho anymore. When it's a battle trying to stay upright, it's not fun anymore.

"I did win it one year," he says of the Hospice race, "but circumstances were different."

Different, indeed. Over the last few racing seasons, Ernie has become a version of the old Cary Grant film *Operation Petticoat*. On the Tuesday night Genesee Yacht Club series, he sails with a crew of four women. They call themselves Ernie's Angels: his daughter Jan Ziobrowski, Mary Ann O'Leary, Mary Finnegan and Jeanie Heil. For the Wednesday evening Rochester Yacht Club races, Ernie and *Desire* are crewed by Jan Anderson and her husband John, and Craig Roth. They range in age from their 40s to their 60s. Ernie calls them "My kids." The kids have watched out for Dad the last couple of years while he's recovered from a few surgeries, including a broken femur. His daughter Jan "treats me like a little kid," Ernie says. "She's been wonderful the past two years while I've been incapacitated. All I had to do was steer and holler.

"One thing I've found out about women, they are very faithful. They don't call up at the last minute and cancel, like some guys do."

But the female crews "have been a training program," he admits. Cranking the jib "takes speed and strength," Ernie insists. "You really need a man on the come-abouts." When racing now, *Desire* and Ernie must rely on his guile. "That's where my experience comes in," Ernie says.

Sailboat racing is strategy. "You've gotta get a good start," Ernie says. "Cut it too cute, and you might end up crossing the starting line early, and be forced to come around and try again. So already you're in last place. When the five-minute gun goes off, you have exactly five minutes to sail to where the starting line is. You have to maneuver around a lot of boats. Check out the other boats. Figure out which is the favorable end, because you want a starboard start. Hit starboard at the high point of the starting line. You could be on a port tack, and another boat is on a starboard tack, and it looks like there's going to be a collision, so the starboard boat has the right of way." This rule of the road was once a matter of economics. Back to England and Ernie's grandparents, and perhaps earlier, as Thames sailing barges loaded with cargo raced each other to the available dock space. "The first boat in got the best prices," Ernie says. Let the lawyers sort out the collisions.

Yeah, it's always lawyers, even for those who seek the solace of water. "You have to know the rules of the road," Ernie says. "There are sea lawyers out there. They win by fouling others up. They like to win by rules, not by skill." Ernie recalls one such scourge with whom he had the misfortune to become entangled during a start. "He cut in front of me, they call it barging. You're not supposed to do that. So I touched him. That's called a collision." A gentle nudge, no damage done, but the sea lawyer went to the Protest Committee afterward. There wasn't much Ernie could say, since his little bit of sailing rage – just letting the guy know he was out of line – had happened right in front of the Protest Committee boat. Apparently, barging is only a gentleman's agreement, while starboard's right of way is the law. Ernie was disqualified.

But sailing is not about the hot wind of post-race disputes. It's about the wind during the sail (Sailors use the word "sail" as a noun, a verb or in the same way a man might announce he is going for a drive). "You've gotta stay in clean wind," Ernie says. "You don't sail behind a boat that's already in there. Stay out in the open. If there's a boat ahead of you, he's using up the air. If there's a boat ahead, it's all disturbed."

It is the rare sail where the boat follows a constant compass line – in sailing it's called the rhumb line. "I never go out to the rhumb line, because there might be a wind shift," Ernie says. "There are times when a rhumb line favors a boat, I would say 20 percent of the time. So you play the averages."

A large amount of data goes into Ernie's computing of those averages. He watches the weather reports, of course. But remember, Ernie comes from an era before The Weather Channel, or local meteorologists bragging about the size of their Dopplers.

He watches the land. Factory and power-station smoke stacks in particular. "If the smoke stacks are blowing, I head to shore," Ernie says. "If the smoke stacks are straight, I head out to sea, because the wind is out there."

He watches the clouds. "It tells me if it's going to rain," Ernie says. "The clouds tell you what direction the upper wind is flowing. When you see clouds, there's usually wind. If they move steady, the surface wind is safe. If they start clearing out, the wind is going to die down."

He watches the water. In light winds, he looks for "cats' paws," ripples of action on the water, indications that there's wind at the surface of an otherwise calm lake. "A little burst here, a little burst there, and you look to see where they are," Ernie says. "Thirty seconds to a minute, then it's gone. There's a lot of luck in sailing in that kind of racing."

And he watches the other boats, before and between races, when the winner is determined by the accumulated finishes over a series of races, as was the case with Ernie's most recent third-place finish. He studies "the leader, or who's closest to me." Only the fastest boat matters. That's whom he's racing. "I ignore the other ones."

Ernie fetches another trophy, for his first-place finish in the 1985 Freedom Cup Race. It's a Plexiglas square with a clock mounted in it. Sailors respect barometers and clocks and such things that measure. It's how they stayed safe, and navigated, for centuries. Sponsored by the Lake Yacht Racing Association, The Freedom Cup was open to boats that were members of yacht clubs on Lake Ontario and Lake Erie. It was a long, overnight race, a real test of a sailor. In this particular year, the course started out of Sodus Bay, east of Rochester, and headed east again to a buoy planted far out in the lake, then west to Rochester, and then back to Sodus Bay. Six divisions of boats, about 10 in *Desire*'s class, each division starting 10 minutes apart.

"I hugged the shore, the rest of the fleet went out to sea," following the rhumb line, Ernie says. "There was a heck of a current that year," as he remembers it, a current that runs from the west to the east, from the Niagara River, curling inward on itself toward the east, before moving on to the St. Lawrence Seaway around Oswego. But this season, the powerful current had left the usual eddy farther west, off Sodus Point. So boats sprinting from the starting line and heading out into the lake were battling that current. Plus, "The shoreline creates friction, and little pockets of wind," Ernie says. Running along the coast at an angle slightly perpendicular to the other boats, he was seeking wind, and finding it, as the other boats drifted with slack sails. By the time he turned *Desire* up into the lake, he'd taken the longer route east but had made much better time.

Now, heading toward the marker set about a mile out into the lake, Ernie could see the other sails far to port, particularly the three fastest boats working upwind. But he could see that their progress was slow. So rather than tacking toward the buoy, he held his course, hoping to get lucky and catch some fresh, clean air. "The wind doesn't completely die out there," he says. "There's always a couple of wind changes."

By keeping his boat on the move, Ernie put himself in position to find those changes. Finally tacking toward the marker, he caught a breeze and rounded his way toward Rochester, with good wind and the current pushing him. The other boats were still straining for the buoy, looking for a breath to fill their sails. But the wind filled Ernie's spinnaker, the sail at the foremast, the one that picks up the boat and really pushes it after the mainsail has done the heavy lifting. "That was the most perfect spinnaker race I ever had," Ernie says of the dash back to the coast.

Now, far out in front, it was getting late. The thoughtful quiet of a boat under full sail settled around *Desire*. Collecting gold pennants makes for a good picture, but....

"I saw the sun set," Ernie says. A larger picture emerges, feeding the romantic soul of men like Ernie. "I saw the moon come up." He was gliding back along the coast, heading toward Sodus Bay with *Desire*, all alone in the darkness, beneath the stars. "I saw the moon disappear." His three crewmen had crawled into the bunks, and Ernie handled the boat by himself. "I saw the sun rise."

Chapter Seven

Perhaps an aging sailor can always enjoy a good sunrise because they looked like that back in 1931 as well. A time when he camped out in swamps and alongside canals, drifting in canoes alongside barges manned by sweating men doing men's work. Stuff that would be an adventure for a 15-year-old boy.

Just before he was to start high school, Ernie and his brother and two friends set off on such an adventure. Ernie and Frank in one canoe, two kids named Donald and Morris in a second, paddling off one morning from the Pittsford canal launch, following the canal south into the Montezuma Marshes. These had been largely drained by the construction of the Cayuga-Seneca Canal, although the water had been restored and the area became a wildlife refuge a few years after Ernie and his entourage passed through. But even before that, "Migratory birds would really load it up," Ernie recalls. The canoeists watched an eclipse of the sun, then glided to Cayuga Lake and on to the Seneca River and into Seneca Lake, portaging their canoes around canal locks, enjoying having much of this to themselves. Tugs cajoled barge loads of oil and grain along the canals. Sometimes it would be a string of six barges, each barge 70 feet in length, an ungainly water train so long that the last barge was for the crew to live aboard. "When they were moving, they used to churn the bottom up because they were so close to the bottom of the canal," Ernie remembers. The two canoes tied up to the tail end of one of these convoys for a night ride on the way back, even passing through the locks with the barges, sometimes stopping long enough for the boys to gather fruit from trees and corn for dinner.

They were gone for two weeks, and Ernie was a couple of days late starting high school. But Ernie does that, shrugs his shoulders at the rules now and then. Miss school a few days? "Sure, why not?" Go AWOL from the Navy? "Sure, why not?"

In fact, his final 22 months of service during World War II, on the Hawaiian island of Maui, evolved into one episode after another of pushing the official envelope. Something about this doesn't sound at all like "the Navy way" that he'd been taught at Great Lakes Naval Station. At Naval Air Station, Kahului, Carpenter's Mate 2nd Class Ernie Coleman was assigned to the carpenter's shop, with duties that included tending to public works projects on the island. Or, since the combat zones were far over the horizon – allowing for a bit of R&R, Rest and Recuperation – there was work "setting up the beer tent," Ernie says, "building shelves and ice boxes where they stored the beer and so forth for dispensing. We put up a couple of small buildings. I learned what a 2x4 was for, and what a 2x10 was for."

Ernie and his fellow Navy carpenters were set up in a warehouse, "open 24 hours, equipped with a stove, stuff like that. Anyone had a problem, they could call us." He started specializing in building shipping boxes. Easy-to-handle, ¼-inch plywood crates held together with big screws, so a serviceman could take a dime edge and fit it into the screw head and easily open the box. "I could knock out one in 15 minutes," Ernie says. Soon enough, they had a little operation set up as well, with Ernie trading the boxes for food, particularly baked goods, "all kinds of pies and cakes." Small things that made war a little easier. Someone even traded Ernie's services for a 1928 Dodge Victory Six, with a starter-generator crank in the front. The only money he ever had to spend on it, to keep it running, was for gas, oil and a $1.21 headlight bulb. Ernie replaced the exhaust system with the steel exhaust pipe from a warplane and made a muffler from a 5-inch shell casing.

Ernie and his fellow carpenters had fashioned a minor pirate kingdom on the edge of the Pacific war "all because I made these shipping boxes in my line of duty," he says.

The winter Kona winds sweeping through the islands, bringing their big rainstorms with them, weren't enough of a disruption to Maui's unrelentingly fine weather. Boring, Ernie has said. Ernie is easily bored. He built himself a surfboard and paddled out into the waves. "There wasn't a lot of surf," he says, but he'd built a window in the board, so at least he could look down into the water.

Possibilities began emerging when Ernie got back into the pleasure-craft shipwright business again. "I must have been talking to one of the guys about building my Snipe," he says of the day his division officer stopped by looking for a bit of a favor himself. "He loved to sail, but he didn't know how to build a boat." Ernie went to work – orders are orders. "We had a pretty good-size lumber yard there," Ernie says, and he soon fashioned a 16-foot dinghy out of white pine, as mahogany wasn't readily available.

That boat wasn't quite big enough for the division officer, so Ernie went to work again, starting with a 20-foot lifeboat, which was a little wider as well. He mounted a mast on it and added a stainless-steel centerboard, since lifeboats don't have the keel necessary for sailing. Cotton for the sail was tough to come by so, "A buddy of the lieutenant at the airfield got me nylon for the sail," Ernie says. It was actually a parachute. "I think I was a pioneer for nylon sails," Ernie says. At war's end, "When I came back, no more cotton sails. They're harder to maintain. Cotton sails need to be dried before you put them away."

This boat was to the division officer's satisfaction, and Ernie used it four or five times himself. While it was a fine diversion for the officers, the boat also proved to be an excellent turtle-hunting craft. Ernie worked at the shop with a couple of Hawaiians – a German and an Irishman, both immigrants – and they knew where to go. With the boat under sail, they'd quietly move into the midst of a group of turtles. Someone would slip into the water and grab onto one. "The turtle wants to go down," Ernie says. "When a turtle's working, it sticks its neck out. The guy takes his knife out" – Ernie makes a slashing motion with an imaginary knife – "it's dead right there." They collected seven or eight turtles during their raid, some weighing 100 pounds, and dropped them off at the Seabees base next door to the Naval Air Station. Ernie was invited to a turtle dinner the next night. "Eleven kinds of meat," he says. "I had the turtle soup. It was very good. Tasted like chicken."

His carpentry skills paid off in other adventures, as Ernie began sampling the American military arsenal. Someone offered him a ride in a submarine. "Why not?" Ernie says. "Well, talk about a boring ride. You climb down in a hole, sit there, feel some tilting. Anyone who was claustrophobic would go ape."

The PT boat was more his speed. "For some reason, they wouldn't tell you how fast we were going," Ernie says. That was probably classified information, so that the Japanese couldn't calculate the boats' movements. "I figured at least 60." Ernie found out later that 65 mph was more like it. "It had five engines hooked to one screw," he says. "Lots of power there.

"And I learned one thing," Ernie adds. When they hit swells, "The chief said, 'Whatever you do, don't stand flat-footed. Bend your knees.'" To this day, that's still how Ernie stands on a boat when it's bounding over swells.

Hitchhiking a ride on a Curtiss SB2C Helldiver was another unauthorized adventure. "Take my place," a Helldiver tail gunner suggested to Ernie one day. "We're just going up for maneuvers."

"Sure," Ernie said. "Why not?"

Maybe not because that SB2C designation to the pilots meant "Son of a Bitch Second Class," due to the plane's beastly handling qualities. A two-man crew operated the Helldiver, with the pilot up front and the tail gunner a good bit behind him in a separate cockpit, facing toward the rear, making it easy enough for Ernie to take the real gunner's place without drawing any attention. All Ernie had to do was sit in the back and watch as the pilot and the rest of the squadron hit a 100-foot island with tiny practice torpedoes. "I never realized G forces were that strong," Ernie says. "At four Gs, your mouth is open, you can't close it, every part of your body is pushing back in the seat."

At 27,000 feet, the pilot radioed back to Ernie, "There's our landing." Ernie looked down. It was an aircraft carrier. "I thought, 'Oh, no, we're not gonna land on that little thing?'" Oh, yes. Having descended, and now scooting along 50 to 60 feet above the waves, "the carrier is higher than we are," Ernie says. "The next time I looked, there wasn't any carrier." It had descended into the trough of a wave. Ernie remembers thinking, "I just hope this guy knows how to land this thing."

He did, and the hook at the tail end of the Helldiver snagged the arresting cable. "It snaps you pretty good," Ernie says. "I had a shoulder strap on, but I almost hit the cowling."

They crawled out of the plane, the pilot looked at Ernie and asked, "Where's Roy?"

"He asked me to take his place."

"Are you a tail gunner?"

"I'm a carpenter's mate."

The pilot shook his head and walked away.

All interesting shenanigans, but they pale in comparison to the weekend that Ernie went AWOL. Absent Without Leave.

It started innocently enough. "A couple of buddies in the barracks," Ernie says, talking about home and wives and girlfriends, and suddenly Ernie was issued a dare: Bet you can't get home to see Ruth. Once again, for Ernie this was a question of, "Why not?"

"One thing led to another, and all of a sudden I'm on a plane."

You needed your own parachute to bum a ride in the Naval Air Force. "You'd better bring it back," his tail gunner buddy said, handing over the chute. Ernie caught a ride to Hickham Field, then talked his way onto a two-engine light bomber, the A-20 Havoc. It's the version outfitted with a Plexiglas nose where the bombardier sat. Since no bombing opportunities would present themselves on this fight, that was Ernie's seat. "Kind of like flying in a patio," he says. Ernie enjoyed a fine view on the flight to San Diego, then cross-country to the Tonawanda airport outside of Buffalo, before taking the bus to Rochester, arriving early Saturday evening.

"What'd you do, get kicked out of the service?" said a shocked Ruth.

"No, just stopping for a visit."

The next morning, Ruth drove him back to the airport. "I caught the same plane back that I came over with," Ernie says. "Nobody knew I was gone." The tail gunner got his parachute back, unused. "It was a stupid thing to do," Ernie says. "If I had gotten stranded, they would have put me in the brig for the rest of the war."

Chapter Eight

You join the Navy to see the world, they say. But they don't give you a guidebook.

With the Japanese surrender in 1945, Carpenter's Mate 2nd Class Ernie Coleman left the Navy as what was called an Inactive Reserve. That meant he could be called back to duty in the advent of some crisis. How long could the planet go without a crisis? Long enough to allow Ernie to be excused from the next one?

Five years. Not long enough. In the summer of 1950, North Korea invaded South Korea. By the spring of '51, Ernie was back right where he didn't want to be. The Navy. Flushing Barracks at the Brooklyn Navy Yard. Where experience was a plus. He was 35 years old, but that was kid stuff. "There was a guy that was 72, called in as a reserve," Ernie says. "Seventy-two years old, and they expect him to go out to sea?"

Maybe if the Navy was re-commissioning Old Ironsides. Still, many of the routines hadn't changed from Ernie's last stretch in the service. If his name wasn't on an assignment roster at 8 a.m. each morning, by 8:01 he and his barracks mates had all of New York City waiting for them. And very quickly, these eager new sailors discovered that you can get something for free, at least as an introductory offer. Heroin. Word spread through the barracks that a free high could be had by servicemen, perhaps as a patriotic gesture.

"You tell the guy, 'Joe sent me,' " Ernie says. "I went with two other guys. I figured, what the hell, why not? I just wondered what the experience was. So he just gives you a shot in the arm" – Ernie simulates a hypodermic going into the veins at the crook of his elbow – "and now I'm a prospective customer."

Turned loose on the streets of New York City with the first-time rush of heroin, they were roaring through the bars and having a big time. "Someone said 'Boo,' everybody laughed," Ernie says. "We were in one bar acting so happy, they threw us out." That was Fifth Avenue.

"That next morning, I woke up with a hangover and a half. Now the trick is, you have to go back and get another fix." Despite his limited experience with narcotics, Ernie knew the next one wouldn't be free. He dealt with the hangover on his own. "It showed me something," he says. "Drugs are not fun."

And soon enough anyway, 8 a.m. came with his assignment: Norfolk Naval Base in Norfolk, Va., to work in the carpentry shop on a training AKA. The Attack Cargo Ship, as these 450-foot holdovers from World War II were known, was designed to efficiently load and unload military cargo at a beachhead. Attack Cargo Ships also transported and launched LCMs – that's Landing Craft Mechanized, the 56-foot-long, shallow-draft barges designed for landing vehicles on a beach – and landing LCVPs. The latter – Landing Craft, Vehicle, Personnel – the famous Higgins Boat, was 20 feet shorter. Turned loose from the Attack Cargo Ships moored offshore in relative safety, they crashed onto the beach, the ramp dropped down into the surf and sand, and troops and vehicles charged out into a hail of machine-gun fire and exploding mortar shells. These landing craft were a common sight at the D-Day landings at Normandy Beach, islands throughout the Pacific during World War II and in a handful of films featuring John Wayne.

And that was the problem on one fatal afternoon that Ernie recalls, during training exercises while anchored about three miles off Morehead City, N.C., a deepwater port with facilities for landing craft. Like the AKAs, the largely wood LCVPs were relics from the war that had ended five years earlier. Ernie's ship dropped one in the water, and the soldiers scrambled down the netting on the side of the ship into the landing craft. But, "The bow logs had rotted," Ernie recalls, "the hinges fell off and the thing went down." As he remembered it, only two men were pulled alive from the water. Twenty men in fully loaded packs drowned.

In the second-guessing that followed the tragedy, "Word got around that I knew something about carpentry and boats," Ernie says. He was put in charge of the crew that inspected the remainder of the landing craft. He found two or three more that had rotted.

Ernie's expertise in repairing these antiquities was greeted with enthusiasm by the ship's captain, who promptly instructed Ernie that his two grandkids back home needed twin beds. Ernie fashioned them in the ship's carpentry shop and was rewarded with a box of Cuban cigars. "And I didn't even smoke," Ernie says.

If heroin didn't give him pause, certainly smoking in 1951 wouldn't be an issue. Ernie joined the smokers hanging out on the ship's fantail one evening. He borrowed a menthol cigarette from a sailor, "took a puff and started to cough," Ernie says. "The guy says, 'That's not the way to start. Take small puffs.' "

The first one was free, but it remained a cheap vice. "Cigarettes were five cents a pack then," Ernie says. "I got hooked."

He'd gotten hooked in another manner of speaking as well. Ernie met Jen Beachner at the Newport Yacht Club's 1948 Turkey Fest. As a teenager, the third of nine girls growing up in Rochester, she had been the 1931 Lilac Festival Queen. "She was a good dancer, and I loved to dance," Ernie says. "Ruth was not a good dancer. So I got to know her well through dancing. She was a very friendly, outgoing person." Jen's husband was a bartender at the club, and when Ernie would go up to the bar for drinks, he'd ask, "Is Jen having a good time?" "I guess so," Ernie would say.

He knew so. "We cheated a couple of times, let's put it that way," Ernie admits. "We had a lot of discussions about a lot of things. She would always listen. Whereas Ruth never did. She always had a word in edgewise."

They went out together as couples, but when Ernie and Jen were alone together, they commiserated on their marriages. "He was a good guy," Ernie says of Jen's husband, a crewman himself on a larger sailboat. "And he was very dull." And Ernie, with that sheen of a newly returned World War II Navy veteran, had some status. "I was the top sailor at the club," he says. "Everyone wanted to know what I did, and learn what I did."

Ernie and Ruth had bought a house on Titus Avenue and were at the center of the Newport Yacht Club social circle. Yachting strangers they'd met in the afternoon were throwing their sleeping bags on the floor that night. "We had a ball," Ernie says. He was also building another Snipe – perhaps with the same goal of manufacturing an excuse to get away from Ruth – while remaining mindful of one basic principle of building a boat in the basement, even when it has a large, exterior walk-in door: "Can I get the boat out without tearing the place apart?" Ernie says. "This happened to one of my buddies. He had to tear apart the foundation to get the boat out."

The Snipe was a beauty, but the distraction it offered didn't save the marriage. Before Ernie was recalled into the service, he asked Ruth for the divorce, and handed over to her the house they'd bought on Titus Avenue and the car. "I left with my tools and my clothes," Ernie says. And he left with one concession from Ruth. The Snipe was about three-fourths finished. "She allowed me to finish the boat," Ernie says.

He calls Jen "the love of my life." Divorce – hers as well, now – cleared the way for that story to continue. When Ernie was assigned to Norfolk, Jen soon followed, renting an apartment and finding a job as a secretary at a furniture company. "If we had maneuvers, I'd be gone for a couple of days," he says. Otherwise, the Korean War was banking hours for Ernie.

As his year's commitment, already extended to 18 months, drew to a close, "The Korean War was getting pretty critical at the time," Ernie says. The fall of 1952 came down to The Battle of Triangle Hill, the bloodiest battle of the year, and would set the conflict on a course of eternal stalemate. Ernie's training ship was sent to the Mediterranean to be closer to the action. But it went without Ernie, who spent his last month of service as a watchman on another AKA quietly docked at Norfolk before he was sent home. He and Jen returned as a married couple, having driven to Elizabeth City, N.C., on a one-day liberty to be married by a justice of the peace. "To make it legal, so to speak," Ernie says. "In those days, people didn't approve of people living together."

Arriving home around Christmastime, their life together in Rochester started with a week living with one of Jen's sisters before they found an apartment on Monroe Avenue. Ernie immediately began working as a carpenter, but when they went on strike he quit the union and began working on his own, taking home-remodeling jobs, building new homes. "Just making money to survive, enjoying what I'm doing," he says. Survival, because unemployed was no way for a newly married man to build a life. Enjoying, because building things is a sense of accomplishment that can be measured. "When a pile of lumber is delivered, and you see an empty basement and all that, and ultimately turn it into a house," Ernie says, "it's a nice, creative feeling."

He doesn't get that same creative feeling at places where he feels "cooped up," as he likes to say. Like Gleason Works. Or a later job at the General Motors parts manufacturing plant on Lexington Avenue. A move he made as a result of that need to make money to survive, and his own restlessness. It wasn't satisfying, either. Watching one machine fold a piece of metal into a tube, a second seal the fold and a third cut it off to the proper length – there, you have a gas line – is not the sort of work enjoyed by a man whose mind is filled with thoughts of sails filling with air.

No, he was better suited to carpentry, and also working on boats at the yacht club, refinishing wood fittings, the kind of thing he was continuing to do at age 93. Jen took another job as a secretary and they found a cottage to rent on Harrison Terrance, in Summerville on the Lake Ontario shore. Over the years, Ernie had been adding skills to his carpenter's bag: plumbing, laying tile, cabinet making, heating. The cottage sat on a large lot, and he not only remodeled it into a year-round residence, but helped build a home on the lot for his new landlords, Jake and Eileen. "I got to be pretty good friends with Jake," Ernie says.

One thing the carpenter hadn't gotten around to building was a family. But when the opportunity presented itself, in 1956, Ernie and Jen became 40-year-old parents. The baby was two days old when Ernie and Jen got her, adopted straight from the hospital.

Ernie's second wife, Jen.

The mother was a friend of a friend, the baby from an adulterous relationship. The transaction was discreet and simple. They named her Patricia, and Jen quit work to take care of her.

Ernie has been forced to rebuild his life repeatedly over his nine-plus decades, in small and large ways. Moving from job to job was a small way. Divorcing Ruth was a big one. Taken separately, each is a life experience, and all too often they are not pleasant moments. These test the will. But gathered up and woven together, each strand becomes a strong rope. The more strands, the stronger the rope. The stronger the character. Perhaps that is how a sailor can look at it. And Ernie was about to weave another strand into the rope.

Pat – Ernie calls her Tricia, sometimes Patti – was 4 years old in 1960. Almost ready for school. Ernie and Jen had gone to bed, but he awoke in the middle of the night, sensing something wrong. He looked over at the twin bed next to him. Jen wasn't there. "I just felt something happened," Ernie says. He got out of bed and walked through the house, and came across a spouse's worst fear: Jen was lying on the living-room floor. "I looked her over, she wasn't there," he says. "I popped on some clothes, ran next door and started hammering on the door, 'Jake, Jen is out, I think she's dead.' " An ambulance was called, but Jen couldn't be revived. Ernie didn't know what it was then, but he knows now: Asphyxiation, due to choking to death on her own vomit. Maybe as a way to make such a death a little more understandable, a little easier to accept, when telling the story Ernie adds as an aside that bandleader Tommy Dorsey also died in this manner. "It's one of those freaky things," he says.

"I was devastated. People said, 'Are you still going to keep Patti?' 'Certainly I am. I'm her father as far as I'm concerned.' "

He lost himself in work, but the hours and hours spent in garages and basements, in search of solace while building boats, wasn't the true Ernie. In fact, he fears being alone. "I don't like myself that much," Ernie says. "In fact, I don't like to go sailing alone. I crave friends."

Yacht club friends helped out. Jake and Eileen next door helped out. Eileen watched Pat while Ernie was at work, and cooked, as did a divorced neighbor with two kids.

And Eileen had an identical twin sister, Evie.

Evie and her husband Gilbert Ross had been a part of the social group with Ernie and Jen, and Jake and Eileen. The Newport Yacht Club was one setting for them, movies another, downtown bars yet another. Jake was in the meat business, and they circulated among the restaurants and bars where he sold prepared hamburger patties and other restaurant meats. "We did a lot of drinking in those days," Ernie says. Gilbert was the kind of guy who would walk into a bar and offer to buy drinks for everyone. That caught up to him. Deeply in debt, deeply depressed, one day he walked into the woods behind his Spencerport house and took his own life.

Evie was left with four kids still at home. Judy was already married and off on her own. But Shirley, Charlie, John and Janice were still at home. Jan was only a few months older than Pat. "Jen would send baskets of food to Evie," Ernie says. On some weekends, Evie would bring the kids up to her sister's house to enjoy the lake.

Maybe you saw this coming. A couple of years after Evie was widowed, just a few months after Jen had died, "I started dating Evie," Ernie says. "Eileen would babysit Tricia. We hit it off very well. She was a wonderful dancer and I loved to dance."

Dancing, just like with Jen. Within the year, Ernie and Evie had married. As with Jen, a justice of the peace handled the paperwork. Ernie's not big on ceremony or lavish events. They moved into Evie's house, which came with a few pluses. Ernie now had a big family, six kids. And it was an interesting house to a fellow in the carpentry trade, particularly one who had built a sailboat from a kit: This was a Bennett Kit Home, similar to the more-familiar prefab Sears Catalog Homes. These houses were delivered as piles of lumber that arrived at an empty basement, just as Ernie was accustomed to seeing, except the pieces were pre-cut and numbered.

There were a few minuses. The railroad tracks were nearby. Probably the same tracks that the house had arrived on. "When a train slowed down, everyone woke up," Ernie says. "At night, you never heard them when they were roaring through."

And with a family to help raise, Ernie sold his Snipe. It seemed there would be no time for racing anymore.

Pat's adjustment was a concern. "When I was alone with her, I pretty much spoiled her," Ernie says. That's if spoiling her was taking his daughter sledding at Durand-Eastman Park, just a short distance from their home on Harrison Terrace, and teaching her how to ride a bike, playing catch and going to the zoo that was once tucked in among the trees of Durand-Eastman. Sounds like normal activities. But once they'd moved from the idyllic Summerville cottage, Ernie nervously got rid of the bike, as their new home was on a busy road. And Pat, who had once been the center of attention, "was no longer the kingpin," Ernie admits.

"She made up for it by being around a big family," he says. And Ernie loved it. He would even draw on his old high-school baseball skills as a backyard catcher for Charlie, a youth-league pitcher.

Ernie was building a new life. But almost without being aware of it at first, he began rebuilding his old life as well. Life on Harrison Terrace with Jen had left him with a longing for the Lake Ontario breezes of Summerville. He felt comfortable there. When a summer cottage at 9 Madison Terrace became available in 1963, just a few streets over from Harrison Terrace, Ernie and Evie bought it and began converting it into a year-round residence.

Two years later, they bought another one just yards away, a few houses from where Madison dead-ends at the beach. Working in his spare time, mostly on weekends, it took Ernie seven years to renovate it to his liking. "How much can you do in one afternoon?" he asks, as though he feels he has to apologize for taking so long.

Enough, given enough afternoons. Ernie created the house he lives in today, with the tiny window with a view of the lake. You can't see the world from there. But you can see the piece of the world that makes sense to Ernie.

Chapter Nine

Most mornings of their married life – 35 years – when Ernie came downstairs before going off to work, the first thing he'd see upon walking into the kitchen was Evie's cigarette, smoldering in an ashtray.

Nothing unusual there. In 1965, 42 percent of Americans smoked cigarettes. Ernie himself had picked up the habit during his second stint in the Navy. But Evie, "She smoked all her life," Ernie says. "She'd get up, the first thing she would do was light a cigarette."

This was an instant decade. Instant coffee. Reach into the pantry, open a can, instant vegetables. American B-52 Stratofortress bombers and Soviet TU-95 Bears would pass each other over Arctic airspace with payloads of nuclear weapons, each intent on their Cold War targets. Instant annihilation. And for Ernie, instant family. Upon marrying Evie in 1961, he and Patti were suddenly living in a very full house.

He wasn't immediately embraced as a family member, Ernie says. The kids had lost their father a few years earlier, and now here was another man moving in, and bringing a 5-year-old with him as well. "It wasn't easy," Ernie says. "The older boy was 13 at the time, he was the father of the outfit. He didn't outwardly reject it. He was a hard kid to talk to anyway."

Nevertheless, "I just loved it," Ernie says. "Evie and I used to have a lot of battles over my discipline. She'd say, 'The kids will never love you.' I told her I didn't care if they loved me as long as they respected me.

"She had an expression, 'If you do that, I'm gonna kill you.' She never killed anybody. I told the kids, 'You lie to me, you're going to pay for it.' Well, one of the kids lied to me. I pulled his pants down, put him over my knee. I didn't hurt him, but he felt it."

Ernie with his third wife, Evie, in 1982.

Ernie was usually out of the house and on his way to a job site by the time the school bus pulled up in front of the house. But he recalls one morning when he was running late, unbeknownst to the two boys, who had stepped behind the house to smoke cigarettes. They would open Evie's cartons of cigarettes from the bottom and slip out a few, figuring she wouldn't notice they were gone. When they heard Ernie come out of the house that morning, they immediately snuffed out their cigarettes, but Ernie knew the game. They were busted. "They asked Evie, 'How come he knows so much about this stuff?' " Ernie says. "She said, 'He was your age once.' "

So it wasn't like Evie and Ernie didn't understand the dangers of smoking.

Taking seriously his new role as head of a populous household, Ernie had sold his Snipe, *Feather*. Too many kids were running around the house for Ernie to waste time sailing. But he and Evie kept his Summerville connection alive after buying that first cottage on Madison Terrace and renting it, even as Ernie renovated it into a year-round home. And they quickly plotted out an unusual arrangement with their renters. As soon as the kids were out of school, the families would swap homes. Evie, Ernie and the kids would spend the summer living on Madison Terrace, with Ernie continuing his renovations. This worked great for a few summers, until the Vietnam War interceded and the renters, conscientious objectors to the war, left for Canada. He was of draft age. The next guy "was a deadbeat, he didn't pay his rent and left a broken-down car in the front yard," Ernie says. "I had to hire a lawyer to get him out of there. He was a headache."

Feather may have been gone, but Ernie wasn't adrift for long. "Sailing is my life," is what he always says. So its return was predictable.

While finishing up a remodeling project, he'd spotted a small home-made sailboat in a garage. That became a part of settling up the bill. Then, on another job, Ernie spotted a Sunfish sitting in a client's garage. The 13-foot sailboat was much smaller and easier to move around than a Snipe. "Never been used," Ernie says. "I offered to buy it from him, he deducted it from the bill and I brought it home. I had the kids in mind."

Truth be told, Ernie may have had himself in mind as well. Although the Sunfish was light enough to run up on the beach at the end of Madison Terrace, Ernie didn't feel comfortable leaving it there. He bought a trailer, rented a garage at a nearby apartment complex and was soon dragging it to yacht clubs up and down the lakeshore, competing in regattas.

In a few years, Jan and Pat got their turn. Easy access to the water brought sailing back into Ernie's life, and now his kids' lives as well, in particular the younger girls. They sailed a one-person Sunfish that Ernie kept on the nearby beach. "You've got to be pretty athletic to sail it. They flip over pretty good," Ernie says. He took the girls out and deliberately dumped the boat, "and showed them what to do, how to get back on board."

Evie never would have stood for that. "She didn't like it when the boat heeled over," Ernie says. "We'd get over five degrees, she'd say, '*Straighten it up.*'"

When the two girls graduated together from Irondequoit High School in 1974, Pat went off to a nearby college, studying two years to be a nurse. "This is a kid who couldn't stand the sight of blood," Ernie says. "Where is she now? The operating room." In Phoenix. Pat had drifted to the Southwest, far from her father's sailing world on Lake Ontario.

But Jan's still here. Ernie had sold the Sunfish and added *Desire* to the family in 1975, and she has been an enthusiastic and increasingly important member of *Desire*'s crew. "I wouldn't be sailing without her," Ernie says. "She fits the boat out in the spring, organizes the crew."

Evie may have been no fan of sailboats heeling in the wind, but the social life of a yacht cub with a solid foundation suited her just fine. A year after buying *Desire*, they joined the Genesee Yacht Club. That was a budget-friendly decision; the Rochester Yacht Club's dues were out of reach for their modest, middle-class income. And there, Evie found a comrade who, like her, didn't like rocking the boat. An outgoing sort, Evie had befriended Paul and Inez Law. Paul had a big 34-foot sailboat, "and he loved to race it," Ernie says. Inez would have no part of that. "She'd sleep on the boat, but couldn't handle the motion when it was moving," Ernie says. "She would drive from one port to the next when we were sailing."

The two women were excellent bowlers as well. Evie even watched it on TV. They dragged their husbands into a mixed Friday night league, where Evie once rolled a 276 game. "Paul tolerated it," Ernie says.

They were out bowling one night when Ernie got a phone call at the lanes. Ruth was dead. She'd remarried, but her husband had died some six months earlier. Ruth had been living alone, and had been found at the bottom of a staircase, apparently having tripped and fallen to her death. "Her sister thought it was foul play," Ernie says quietly. He does not seem to be a conspiracy theorist.

As Ernie returns to Evie's story, retelling it in the fall of 2010, he adds that five days earlier he'd been at Inez Law's funeral. She died of a brain tumor.

The older you get, the deeper grows the warehouse of souls. It took a decade for the final drama of Evie's life to unfold, but a lifetime of smoking caught up with her. Evie's doctor tried to head it off, ordering her to quit in 1985. Ernie stopped smoking as well, "because she had to," he says. "I really missed it. It was difficult. I used to bum a cigarette every so often for a while."

The pressure in Evie's left eye grew increasingly elevated however, and four operations couldn't save it. The retina detached, and she went blind in that eye. "Nobody knew it," Ernie says. "She did a good job of hiding it."

They were looking into getting Evie a glass eye when, after ignoring some nagging concerns, she finally went for a mammogram. Maybe all of the drama of her eye troubles had been enough to keep her from pursuing more bad news. But Evie "kept putting it off," Ernie says, "because she was afraid she had cancer."

Unfortunately, Evie was right. Ernie took her in at 9 in the morning. They didn't get home until 10 that night. Her mammogram had shown a dark spot on a lung. Returning to Rochester General Hospital, doctors went for a biopsy through her back, inadvertently collapsing a lung in the process, and Evie spent a few days in the hospital attempting to recover. The tests came back in two weeks, confirming the tumor was malignant.

Still, her doctors said, she had a 95 percent chance of survival.

Radiation treatment is scary business now, and it was doubly so in 1995. "Radiation kills the cancer cells," Ernie says. "It also kills the cells around it. The scar tissue collected around her lungs." That meant her lungs' ability to process oxygen was being compromised.

With each disappointing visit to her doctors, it was becoming clearer that Evie would be among that five percent of non-survivors. While she was being treated, Ernie would stand outside the hospital, watching others. "People were under the canopy, smoking like a chimney," he says. "And they were all working there! I still see them up there smoking, when I have the occasion to go there. Smoking in their white outfits."

Evie was on oxygen now, "cords all over the house," Ernie says. She was suffocating. "She was never in any pain, pain from the cancer. She had anxiety attacks, because she couldn't catch her breath."

Ernie had set her up in a hospital bed in the first-floor family room that he'd added on to their home, the renovation that had been a part of the plan for spending their lives together. "I rigged up a bell system so she could reach up and press a button when I wasn't in the room," he says. "I had another bell downstairs in the shop." Hospice workers had been coming for a couple of hours every day. Judy would spend every Tuesday with her mother. "I needed it. It was rough," Ernie says. "I needed that four hours to myself."

Evie fell into a coma her final two days. "I thought, 'She's gonna die of starvation,' " Ernie says.

Evie's oldest son Charlie, his wife Betsey and their youngest daughter Kate were with her when Ernie went for a walk. "They hollered, 'Come on back!' " Ernie recalls. He was too late. "She died with her eyes wide open," Ernie says. "That really bothered me. We had to close them."

Chapter Ten

Ernie's man cave is beneath his home on Madison Terrace. It's a small basement, partitioned into three rooms, although that's a little hard to tell with all the lumber leaning this way and that, like sailors still in search of their land legs. But the shop begins to make sense as you poke about in the dingy, worn light. Details emerge. Over there, lines for *Desire*, looped and knotted in nautical ways. Here, a drill press. Table saw. Band saw. Vices. Dust. Wood trim, with a loop of twine at each end, hangs from the ceiling. Shelves overloaded with cans of paint and solvents, who knows how old some of that stuff is? In the wood floor joists overhead, Ernie has nailed the tin lids from baby-food jars. He fills the jars with screws and nails, then twists the jars back into their lids, where they hang like bats. This shop is the sum of little tricks that Ernie has picked up from all of the carpenter shops that he has been in over the years.

"Here's a project I'm working on for a client," Ernie says, holding up a child's tiny rocking chair. It looks like an antique. It's old, anyway. Ernie will sand it, stain it, varnish it and make sure the joints fit nice and tight. Whenever he gets around to it. You get the feeling that, by now, the kid for whom that chair was intended is getting a little too big to fit in it.

Ernie appreciates the final result of his labors. But he is more enamored of the process. "Get a truck, dump a bunch of lumber and it ends up a house," is one of the ideas that he's fond of. "Same with building a boat. Get a bunch of lumber, and it floats."

He had the magic hand early when it came to building Snipes, the racing class that first caught his eye while he watched a trio of the boats from California dominate the Newport Yacht Club races in

Ernie sitting in his first Snipe, *Kiddo*, in 1947.

Irondequoit Bay in the mid-1930s. His first, *Kiddo*, launched his racing career, his success on Irondequoit Bay prompting him to dip his toe into foreign waters. World War II was on, as was gasoline rationing, so Ernie tucked a 20-gallon drum of gas into *Kiddo*'s cockpit and latched the boat trailer onto the back of the 1940 Plymouth convertible he'd just acquired from a guy who'd joined the Navy. "He told me, 'If you make the payments, you can have the car,' " Ernie says. "He still owed $300 on it, so I considered that a pretty good deal." He and Ruth piled in with another couple from the Newport Yacht Club, John and Esther O'Brien, and made the 300-mile drive to the North Atlantic Snipe Class Championships on Lake Mohawk, a large artificial body of water in New Jersey.

As Ernie immediately discovered, "It was similar to the bay, which I knew like the back of my hand." He would be racing against 16 other boats, and upon his arrival was informed that there was a home-water favorite. "They all told me, 'Oh, Beckett's going to win. You came all of the way from Rochester to get beat by Beckett?' "

Beckett. Ernie never did learn the man's first name, but did get a sense of what he was going against. "He'd have his lackey bring his boat over," Ernie says. "Then he'd drive over in his Cadillac."

Ernie won the first race on Saturday. "I played the wind," he says. "I watched the trees and the clouds." After winning the day's second race, he was pulling his boat from the water to let it dry out for Sunday's third and final race. "They said, 'Oh, you can't pull your boat out of the water,'" Ernie says. These were the local wharf rats, stunned that the mighty Beckett was being shut out on his home waters. Ernie ignored them and pulled his boat. The race committee checked out *Kiddo*, this mysterious alien craft, measuring its dimensions, measuring its sails. But everything fell within Snipe parameters.

That last race, "Everybody ganged up on me," Ernie says. "There was hardly any wind. But I thought, if there was going to be any, it looked like it was going to be coming from the stern." He was right. Laying back, "I caught the wind and sailed around the whole fleet," he says. "It was very exciting for a country bumpkin to go down there and beat all of these doctors and lawyers from New York City." And he did it with another affront to the home boys' manhood. On these two-man boats, Ernie's crewman had been a woman, Esther O'Brien. Her husband, and Ruth, came along for the party.

Weeks later, Ernie and *Kiddo* went their separate ways. He sold the boat and joined the Navy.

While off in the Pacific, Ernie pondered the intricacies of boat building, which he put in practice upon his return. "I had the idea that it was a little too blunt," he says of the bow. Using the kit frames, he slid the second and third frames back an inch apiece, making for a narrower bow. The front piece of the bow was hard oak, to fend off whatever he might encounter floating in the water. But the rest of the boat, "I built it out of very soft wood, western cedar, what they make shingles out of," Ernie says, "because it was light and available."

Diplomatically named *R's* – although Ruth wouldn't be spending a lot of time aboard it – he tweaked his second Snipe until it screamed. This craft was aching to be measured against the best, and in 1946 that meant the Nationals, that year being held in the Gulf of Mexico, off of Corpus Christi, Texas. Ernie and three other guys in a Buick Roadmaster stacked their two boats – *R's* and *Ghost* – one on top of the other on a trailer for the 1,775-mile ride to Texas.

Early in the drive, the weight of the boats proved to be too much for the trailer and it began to fold in on itself lengthwise. They bought some chains, cinched it up as tight as they could, stopping every now and then to tighten it a little more, until they'd drawn the trailer back to a pretty close approximation of what they'd started with. Ernie drove the final dusk-to-dawn shift. He still remembers those long stretches of Texas road, interrupted only by bumps where the railroad tracks crossed, until the diamond lights of Gulf Coast oil refineries drew them in to Corpus.

This was a land of extremes. Sun, wind and waves. "The local boys had coveralls on and hats with a skirt on the back," Ernie recalls. "They were covered. I had a good tan, but I got sunburned on top of it."

The Nationals, once again, were to be a series of three races, with 50 boats nosing toward the starting line. "Very windy," Ernie says. "Extremely windy. The boat in front of me capsized. I'd see it and then it was gone.

He was in the trough, I was on the wave. I just missed one guy in the water. Those centerboards are as sharp as a knife, you know.

"I was doing very well. Until the last race. I crossed the starting line one second early." Ernie had to circle back and start again. He needed to place 20th or better to finish third overall. From dead last, he managed to climb back to 30th. Not good enough. *R's* was 10th overall. Nevertheless, "I was very pleased," Ernie says. "It was really rough." Later that summer, after a fourth-place finish in a big set of races at Chautauqua Lake, he sold *R's* on the spot to a guy from New Jersey.

Ernie went to work in the basement on his third Snipe. More tinkering, and squabbling. But nothing was going to get in the way, including asking Ruth for a divorce in the midst of the project. "I built it extra light, because weight was important," he says. The hull was ½-inch cedar once again, rather than oak; the deck ¼-inch plywood. He left the cockpit opening extra large, further reducing weight. "The weight was below the waterline," Ernie says. "The weight" – or absence of weight – "above the waterline is very important. The more water you displace, the more you have to push out of the way with your sail."

He named it *Feather*. As in, light as a feather.

"Boy, that boat was hot," Ernie says. It was also too light for the Snipe class. Ernie had nearly outsmarted himself. Oak floorboards and a bronze centerboard added the necessary 30 pounds, keeping him in fleet championship trophies, until he married Evie. As he tells the story of his boats now, *Feather* is the only one that he knows is still afloat today, cruising the lakes in Kansas.

Ernie has said that *Desire*, the boat he's had for nearly four decades, is not really a racing boat. But he sails it like it is. And *Desire* sails like it wants to be one. "It acts like a Snipe," he says. "It has a big jib and a high boom. That's a Snipe configuration right there.

"And, it's unforgiving, like a Snipe. You make a mistake, you're out."

Someone on another boat has taken a photo of *Desire*, winning a race in the fall of 2010 series. Yes, at age 93, Ernie is still winning his races. Pointing to the photo, he shows how his all-woman crew is doing the work. One handles the foresail, the triangular sail at the front of the boat, fixed to a line that runs from the top of the mast to the bowsprit.

Another handles the mainsail, which trails behind the mast. Two others are in the cockpit with Ernie, dealing with lines, the tiller and other tasks.

"You watch the curl," Ernie says, pointing to the edge of *Desire*'s white jib. Sloops can wear different styles and sizes of foresails, each designed for a different wind: jib, spinnaker and the extra-large jib, a genoa. The photo shows that *Desire*'s jib does have a barely perceptible curve outward, near the wide top. That means the sail's full, catching all of the wind that it can. "Like a balloon," Ernie says. "It needs constant attention."

Now he points out the thin black line running the length of the hull, where it meets the water. That's the bootstripe. "Always, when I'm sailing, I try to keep it on a level line," he says. "With the spinnaker out, it tends to push the bow down. You want the boat level fore and aft. If the bow is buried, you're not making progress. If the stern is buried, you're not making progress." Ernie watches a set of levels in the cockpit, to make sure the boat is perfectly balanced. Sometimes he has to move the crew members around, using their weight as counterbalances to get it right.

In the photo, the bootstripe is one steady line from bow to stern. *Desire* is perfectly balanced.

What looks like ski poles project from either side of the mast, low enough so that the mainsail boom will sweep over them. These are wind compasses that Ernie added in 1990. Compasses high on the mast – and Ernie has those as well – may be misleading. "The wind can vary, 10, seven, eight miles an hour from the top of the mast to the bottom," he says. "There's more wind higher off the water. I go up 36 feet." And on the mainsail, unlike what's happening up front with the foresails, it's the wider bottom that's catching the most wind, giving the boat the most push. *Desire* is a complex piece of machinery. Ernie reads the compasses, the cockpit levels, the telltales dangling from the lines and the look of the sails to gauge how efficiently *Desire* is moving.

In building Snipes, he tweaked this, tweaked that, found the extra speed. Even though *Desire* was ready to sail from the moment he got his hands on the boat in 1972, Ernie couldn't resist tweaking yet again, and again. It's an obsession, as he evolved into a craftsman sizing up each boat in front of him, pondering what he could do to make it better. Tweaking boats has been his profession for the past decade. He stopped being a carpenter long ago. It's been years since he cut a board in someone else's employ. "I'd decided I'd had enough. I went in for myself," he says. "Boat repair, because there was plenty of it."

His bad knees won't allow him to get down on the deck anymore, doing the tough work, but he can sit on a stool and work with those wood fittings, sanding and varnishing until they shine. Or repair a ding in the fiberglass so it matches the original surface. He is a crafty creature emerging from the cavern beneath his home on Madison Terrace with a vial of alchemy, some sandpaper and an idea of what it can be. It is a metaphor for how he's shaped his life, and everything around it, for 93 years. Perhaps that boat was once a beauty, but now needs a little tender loving care. Ernie understands it. "Think of a blonde," he says, "with a few teeth knocked out."

The life had gone out of the house on Madison Terrace. Evie had died, and Ernie's response was to move all of the furniture aside in the back room, the one where she had spent her final days. He threw blankets over everything and set up a net against one of the walls.

"I covered the west window with heavy cardboard, and I would practice golf by the hour," he says. Whiling away the time, hitting one golf ball, then the next, then the next. He did this for months. His daughter Judy came to visit.

"This looks like a bachelor's pad," she said.

"Well, I guess it is," Ernie said.

But by February of 1996, the bleakness of the Rochester winter was squeezing Ernie like a fist. He closed up the house and drove to Florida, visiting friends and his brother Frank, "to get away from the boredom, too." He played a little golf, although the indoor sessions had hardly raised him to touring-pro level. "If I break 100, I'm happy," he says. When he returned to Rochester, "I buried myself in work. Seven days a week. Painting bottoms, waxing hulls, doing varnish work."

But by June, he knew: "I can't stand this living alone. I'm not a guy for living alone. I like company."

He began reading the classified section of the newspaper. The personals. "You just look down the list, 'Women Wanting Men,' " he says. Just like buying a car or some tools. "I found one that said 'I like skiing and sailing,' something like that. So I answered the ad.

"Marilyn called, said she'd like to meet me, and we set a date to have coffee. Half an hour later, she called back and said, 'Why don't you just come to the house?' "

Marilyn's 30-year marriage had fallen apart a couple of years earlier. After a year of feeling sorry for herself, she'd started moving on with her life, trying singles groups such as Parents Without Partners. But with no success. So she went to the personals. This direct-marketing approach worked fine in one respect. Marilyn received 28 responses.

But the quality of the pool left something to be desired. The first 27 didn't measure up in one respect or another. Everyone was carrying some kind of baggage. Except, perhaps, this last one, Ernie. He had potential. Her ad had said she was looking for a first mate. He had a boat, and an interest in learning how to ski.

Ernie showed up at her house with a bottle of red wine and a bottle of white. Marilyn did a quick evaluation when she answered the door. He was kind of sailorish in appearance, with his white beard and mustache, wearing what she calls "a funny Greek sailing cap." And he didn't seem to fall within the age range that her ad had called for, 55 to 65. He was to the December side of that. Nevertheless, she let him in. Didn't want to hurt his feelings.

"She talked me into cooking steaks," Ernie says. "By midnight, the wine was gone. I was a mellow fellow. I took my time driving home.

"She was so friendly and so outgoing. I was impressed."

They quickly became friends. And friends was all they could be, Marilyn warned Ernie. The age difference was too daunting.

After a few evenings of chili or stew at his house, Ernie made the big move. "I asked her, 'How would you like to go sailing on *Desire?*' " From there, "Every date we had was to go sailing." Ernie had the wind at his back now. He knew she was much younger than he. Fifty-five, in fact. "I didn't tell her I was almost 80," he says. "She didn't ask me."

Marilyn strolls into the kitchen where Ernie's sitting at the table discussing their courtship. "All the guys I was dating ended up being such losers," she says. "So I always ended up coming here. That must have told me something."

The sailing season was coming to a close that first year of their relationship, and Ernie's kids were planning on celebrating his birthday on Nov. 20. Ernie was plotting otherwise. In her job as a travel agent, he knew Marilyn was putting together a singles cruise for a local ski club that would have her gone during his birthday.

"Think there's room for me?" he asked.

"Dead silence...."

She didn't have the heart to tell Ernie that he was too old for a singles cruise. Even if the singles were in their 50s and a decade beyond that. She relented.

"I called up the kids, postponed the party for a week," Ernie says. "That's when she found out how old I was, when I told her my kids were planning an 80th birthday party for me."

Marilyn's reaction?

Ernie smiles. " 'Gulp....' "

He'd faced long odds in the past. This would be yet another challenge. And on the cruise Ernie showed he was up to the job once again. "We were on the ship with all of these young guys, and by 9 they're in the sack asleep, or whatever," Ernie says. "I'm up there dancing. I guess she was impressed with that. She told me later, 'Somehow, you managed to turn that around.' Anyway, it was a happy ending."

Ernie wasn't done. At 80, he took up skiing as well. After six lessons, he was hitting the intermediate trails. "I'd always wanted to ski, but I couldn't afford it," he says. "But the kids were gone, and I was alone now. And I really loved it. She dragged me out to Jackson Hole, Wyo. I enjoyed it. I didn't do anything crazy."

After three years on the slopes, Ernie had to hang up the skis. Doctor's orders; too rough in his aging knees and heart. "Giving that up was the hardest thing I had to do," he says.

Yet on other fronts, the relationship was progressing nicely. Ernie was proving to be a durable travel partner on the trips arranged by his travel-agent girlfriend Marilyn.

And one weekend, rather than bothering going home, Marilyn simply stayed at Ernie's. "I thought, 'Oh wow, this is interesting,' " Ernie says. By late in the spring of '97, "She started spending every weekend here. Things were getting better and better."

Now it was Ernie's turn to set some parameters. "I told her I'm not looking for marriage," he says. "I'm a jinx. I married three women. I don't want to put that curse on a fourth."

Nevertheless, he began converting an upstairs bedroom into an office for Marilyn. "Her ivory tower," he calls it, where she could do telemarketing work. Before long, "She moved in with me," he says. "The kids all approved. I also told them I was spending their inheritance. They said they didn't need it, anyway."

Ernie and his fourth wife, Marilyn, on the slopes at Jackson Hole, Wyo.

So the old folks were shacking up. "It was kind of her idea, I think," Ernie says. "She needed some kind of security. I'm an old geezer. What if I pass away? So one day I said to her, 'Let's get hitched.' Then I thought, 'That's a hell of a thing to say.' "

He tried again. " 'Sweetie, would you marry me?'

"The next day, I went out and bought her an engagement ring. She picked it out."

After a five-year courtship, they were married on Oct. 20, 2001. In what was Ernie's well-practiced routine, they went to a justice of the peace. "Love, honor and obey," Ernie says. "Well, strike that obey."

The next month, they had a combination wedding reception and Ernie's 85th birthday party at the Rochester Yacht Club, with 177 guests. "Charlie had an SUV there to bring the stuff back to the house, and it was loaded," Ernie says. "It took us two days to go through it. Needless to say, there was a lot of booze. We didn't need to buy anything for six months."

Chapter Twelve

"Flyboys," he calls them. Ernie remembers standing outside the Maui base one beautiful clear morning watching a group of seven of them – "They were young kids" – hot-rodding over the landscape in their Grumman F6F Wildcat fighters, perhaps 20 miles distant, soaring straight toward the Haleakala volcano. "All seven of them didn't pull up quickly enough," Ernie says. "You could see them trying to pull up, but they were following the leader." His hand becomes the flight path of each fighter plane, soaring and abruptly ending on the side of Haleakala. "It was like watching a movie," he says. "Nobody made it."

A call came in to the carpenter's shop a few hours later. The bodies had been recovered, seven rough boxes were needed. The carpenters called a guy out of the brig, a common practice when they found themselves shorthanded. You just had to promise you were going to bring him back. Ernie had the prisoner lie down on a 4x8 sheet of plywood so he could trace out a basic coffin shape. When the guy figured out what was going on, he leaped to his feet in fear. He wasn't going to be used as a template for death.

This memory probably goes back to 1944. Thirty-one years later, in 1975, Ernie returned to Hawaii. He was 55 years old. Who knew how much time he had remaining on the old clock? He chose Hawaii, he says, "to see the place where I spent 22 months. Show Evie all about it."

And perhaps to remember that he had once been a part of something that was really big. He'd been a player in important history. One of those "Greatest Generation" guys that the TV news anchor Tom Brokaw likes to talk about.

They flew to Honolulu in a 747, "the first time I ever saw one," Ernie says. "Boy, the engines on that thing. They're monster things." He heard tell of a mystical second level in that aircraft, up a spiral staircase at the front of the plane where other passengers enjoyed their cocktails as they soared 30,000 feet over the Pacific Ocean. Ernie was just a guy who fixed boats so, "needless to say, we didn't go First Class."

But they were first-class tourists. They peered into Mauna Loa, the world's largest volcano, on the Big Island of Hawaii. "It was bubbling at the time we were there," Ernie says. The chances of Ernie and Evie getting roasted were unlikely, as Mauna Loa's eruptions are quite mild. Yet, "The smell of sulfur was horrible," he says. "They didn't let you stay long. You would be asphyxiated."

The island of Maui, where he'd spent his time, was of more interest. Ernie's recollection of the old whaling port of Lahaina from his Navy days was that there weren't any whales to be seen. Many years later, he'd heard on a Jacques Cousteau TV documentary that fish won't come within 100 miles of water where dynamite has been exploded. "Since it's only 90 miles from Pearl Harbor," Ernie says of Lahaina, "there was a lot of dynamite in the water." But in 1975 Ernie saw that whale watching was a big industry in Lahaina. All had been forgiven between nature and the planet's angry inhabitants, at least in that pleasant corner of the world. "Apparently the ocean cleared it up," he says.

The memories were thicker still around Haleakala volcano, deep in dormant slumber, its old lava flows wrapped around it like a blanket. During the war, this is where sailors were sent for Rest and Recuperation. And target practice. "They wanted us to shoot the goats," Ernie says. "They were propagating so badly, they were coming out of the crater and eating the pineapples." Ernie recalled for Evie how he and four of his Navy pals packed three days' worth of food and hiked up to the ranger cabins. At the 10,000-foot summit, they could look down into the valley and watch the flyboys scooting low along the valley at the foot of the mountain, the Wildcats literally at their feet. "They were a pretty good match for the Zero," Ernie says, referring to the Japanese fighters, "because they were maneuverable. The F4s too, but they added heavier armaments to the F6." As usual, Ernie knows his specs.

He and his fellow goat squad members were told it would be cold on Haleakala, and that proved to be true. Ernie remembers waking up the first morning and blowing on his eyeglasses, hoping to raise a little condensation so that he could clean them off. But even though he saw a thin layer of ice on top of the rainwater-collecting barrels at the ranger cabins, "you couldn't even see your breath, that's how dry it was up there." At these elevations, and only on the Hawaiian volcanic summits of Haleakala and Mauna Kea, grows the beautiful silver-green colored silver sword. Ernie noticed that the narrow leaves on one silver sword, which bloom in an exotic ball, were moving in an odd way. Poking about, he discovered that air was blowing out of mysterious holes in the long-hardened lava. Tubes big enough to admit a man, formed as the lava had cooled.

For a kid who'd tested himself time and again against what Lake Ontario had to offer, this was too exotic a sight to resist. "I said, 'You want to go down there? I want to see what this is all about.' " With flashlight beams pointing the way, Ernie led two of the guys into the tube, which soon expanded into a space the size of the kitchen where he was sitting now, recalling this adventure. "I told them, 'No hollering, or it might fall on us." Such channels feed the lava flow itself. When an eruption ends, the lava drains back down the slope and into the volcano, leaving the tubes clear. And these tubes can be extraordinarily long. One of Mauna Loa's is 31 miles.

They kept pushing farther into the volcanic passage, perhaps 150 yards. Even there, Ernie could still feel a breeze blowing from the tube. But it had grown too narrow and they were forced to turn back.

There was a massacre to tend to, anyway. The Navy men took their carbines into the crater and someone spotted a goat peering over a steep cliff. Everyone opened fire. "I'll bet that head had 15 shots in it," Ernie says. "You'd think it was a battle up there."

They were just young guys, cutting loose after experiencing the worst that humanity can offer, war.

But some of Ernie's images of R&R on Maui were unsettling. He has a memory of the 4th Marines returning from Iwo Jima, and how a handful of them went on rampage, killing nine Japanese-American civilians, "because they were trained to kill Japanese," Ernie says. "They had to be quarantined, to straighten those guys out. It was horrible."

For the first half of his life, adventure abroad came infrequently for Ernie, considering his heavy schedule of renovating houses and boats, sailing, wearing a gorilla suit to scare the neighborhood kids on Halloween and, after marrying Evie, raising a big family. His travels had generally been modest or government-subsidized. Big vacations were an irresponsible use of time and money for a Great Depression kid. But as he began to reach out and explore the world, his excursions were never far from water.

He took his first cruise in 1969 aboard *Rotterdam*. "When the ship was the old rules," Ernie says. "If you didn't have a tux on for the Captain's Dinner, you don't go." The seven-day voyage left New York City and motored through Cape Hattaras down to Freeport, Nassau and Bermuda. It was a Dutch ship. "All they had on board was Heineken," Ernie says. He's not complaining. "Seven-point-five cents a glass. I don't know where they got the half-cent. All you had to do was tell them your cabin number."

This kind of life went down easy with Ernie. Friends like Bill and Barb, an English couple who house sat for them, helped ease his mind about being away from home. True, "Bill went out one night and the dog wouldn't let him back in," Ernie says. But that was forgiven. Their friends eventually moved back to England, and Ernie regrets not taking them up on an offer to visit. "I never got around to it, seeing my heritage," he says. "I'll probably never see England."

Instead, Ernie and Evie tried cruises to Puerto Rico in 1980, and another in 1991 on *Pacific Princess* through the Panama Canal. That canal still rankles the casual historian in Ernie. "We built the thing, then we gave it away," he says severely. For fans of gentle irony, it was while on *Pacific Princess*, the original star of the mid-1970s through '80s TV series *The Love Boat*, that they heard the news that the U.S. had invaded Iraq.

But after he turned 80 in 1996, Ernie emerged as a true globe-trotter. Marilyn had organized tours to all sorts of exotic destinations. Even before they married, Ernie had started tagging along. Places like the Dominican Republic, where Marilyn hired a pilot with braces on his teeth to fly a helicopter up and down the beach while she scouted potential resorts for her clients. Antigua, where Ernie got involved in the resort's daily Hobie Cat competitions on the beach, winning every race with the small catamarans. His prize: a bottle of rum. There were two weeks in Italy, which he fell in love with. Then Germany, Austria and Switzerland. They did Tahiti and the Polynesian islands – "very hot, not much to see," Ernie says dismissively. And cruises to St. Maarten, Venice, Croatia, Greece, Majorca, Tunisia, Barcelona, France and Alaska, which also required hops on a helicopter and seaplane. There was Sedona, Ariz., beautiful in its rocky landscape and artist studios. And the ski trip to Jackson Hole, Wyo.

Now there would be no more skiing, on doctor's orders. And it was while riding a train to the Matterhorn, at about 9,000 feet altitude, that Ernie realized he couldn't breathe, forcing a retreat by train down to 6,000 feet. With worldliness comes age. Recently, Ernie has needed a wheelchair to get through airports in a timely fashion.

But alternatives are at hand. In 2008, they discovered *Royal Clipper*, the largest sailing vessel in the world, manned by a crew drawn from countries throughout Europe. It's Lord Nelson meets *The Love Boat*, with three swimming pools. Morning gymnastics with Maria, Captain Sergey's Story Time on the bridge, snorkel safaris with the Sports Team, land excursions to Mount Etna ("please wear comfortable, closed shoes"), dolphin watching with marine biologist Clara, mast climbing with the Sports Team, compulsory lifeboat drill, deck golf with the Sports Team, and Cocktail Melodies with Tanya and Kunya followed by Pirate Night in the Tropical Bar ("Come dressed as a pirate ready for dinner"). All guided by state-of-the-art navigation equipment.

"And the food?" Ernie rolls his eyes and rubs his belly. When you're raised in the Great Depression, extravagant food must still look like a miracle. "If you go away hungry from that place, it's your own fault," he says. "I took fish every time. Salmon, mahi mahi, sea bass, flounder, grouper. The desserts, I gained three pounds in two days. I had to stop eating dessert, my belt was getting too tight. The last night, they came out with baked Alaska, parading around with it, candles and so forth."

Ernie at the helm of *Royal Clipper* in 2008.

This was a vacation that appealed to the old sailor, and perhaps his cardiologist, who was concerned about his patient scampering around on the ruins of ancient civilizations. "Needless to say, I got my sea legs back after two days," Ernie proudly says. "I'm walking a straight line, and they're staggering."

Ernie and Marilyn returned to the ship in 2009 and 2010. Their third voyage on *Royal Clipper* was seven days noodling around the Mediterranean. "This is Italy, theoretically," Ernie says, having sketched out a map on a legal pad. He'll never make it as a cartographer, but it's all there: Naples, the Tyrrhenian Sea, the Aeolian Islands with their two active volcanoes, Sardinia and the Strait of Messina, the 1.8-mile waterway between Sardinia and the boot of Italy. "They're talking about building a bridge over that," he says.

Since his heart condition began emerging, "I can't travel very far," Ernie says. "If I walked from here to the end of the street" – that's about 150 yards – "I'd have to stop." But from the boat he could gaze at sights such as Italy's Amalfi Coast, once a vacation spot for royalty. "Of course, now it's a tourist trap," Ernie says. "How those Italians build on the side of those mountains, I don't know. It's 1,200 steps to their houses, can you imagine carrying groceries up there?"

Ernie appreciates such industrious aspects of humanity. He doesn't look much like a Fascist but, he says, admiringly, "Mussolini did an awful lot with that country to modernize it."

For Ernie, *Royal Clipper* is a marvel. He toured the engine room below, a miracle of cramped engineering. Three diesel engines, if the wind has another assignment at the moment. But overhead is the true breathtaking sight. Five masts filled with 42 stunning white sails, including the nine elegant staysails. "They stick out like a jib off the main mast," Ernie explains. "Of course, when we were going downwind, the staysails aren't doing anything. They're just decoration. People took pictures anyway. It had the effect."

He watched the more-daring sailor tourists climb a mast into the crow's nest. "They put a belt on you, so if you misstep you don't fall in the drink," Ernie says. He watched a young female member of the crew scamper up the mast to the highest yardarm, then walk out onto it, taking photographs. "I thought, 'This girl is crazy.' "

As Ernie has said, no two sails are alike. Nor are they equal. On that third voyage, sails as decoration and masts as a gymnastics venue weren't enough for Ernie. "I wasn't too thrilled with this one," Ernie says. Not enough wind for good sailing meant the diesels were running too much. "There were areas we couldn't sail because we headed into the wind. We had to motor." A steady, if not-too-thrilling, 11½ to 12 knots.

Still, much like a golfer for whom one or two nice shots over 18 holes is encouragement enough to return to the course, Ernie returns to *Royal Clipper* in search of the miracle of his first voyage. Departing Barbados, with stops at Granada, St. Lucia and St. Vincent. The captain even let Ernie take the helm for a half hour.

But what he remembers most are those first moments, leaving port about 5 p.m. They were about 8 to 10 miles out, cruising at 5 or 6 knots. The sun was sliding away over the horizon, and Ernie began to notice the music being played on speakers throughout the ship. It was Vangelis' overture for the film *1492*, and *Royal Clipper* was catching the wave swells in perfect time to the music's swells.

"The sails started coming down. Oh, it was breathtaking," Ernie says. "You can't explain it, you have to experience it. I think about it, it brings tears to my eyes. It was one of the most memorable moments in my life."

Chapter Thirteen

Ernie's lesson of the new millennium: Your odometer doesn't hit the eight-decade mark without things going wrong. Ernie was discovering that in a big way now.

Even the parties were getting dangerous. The tourists at an Antiguan resort were being encouraged to participate in a game where a guy sits with a balloon on his lap and, in what must surely be a great blow to personal dignity, his partner bounces on him and attempts to break it. Ernie and Marilyn, in Antigua on a 2004 travel-agent junket, were pulled into the competition. "She jumped on my lap and pushed me right over," Ernie says.

He knew immediately something had happened to his back. "I wasn't going to have an X-ray there," he says, wary of exposing himself to the care of anyone but American doctors. "I laid down for an hour and I couldn't get back up."

That would remain the pattern when Ernie returned to Rochester. He was forced to sleep sitting upright on the couch, his feet stretched out on an ottoman. He tried physical therapy and a chiropractor. "Nothing worked," Ernie says. "We were considering acupuncture. We had a name of a guy and everything."

Although, oddly, he could still play golf.

This was a new way of life, and Ernie accepts it. "I had never had a broken bone or anything," he says. "I never even took an aspirin, even if I had a headache. I was not a pill popper."

He shrugs. "Now I'm taking them all the time. It keeps me going. I'm not about to stop now."

Ernie's brother, four years older, is still puttering along in a lucid manner in his Florida apartment. He hated the New York weather, and moved to Florida for the year-round golf. But now, "I'm no longer physically able to swing a golf club," Frank complains. At 98, his mind seems reasonably solid, although he can't remember how many times he's been married. "Let's see, twice maybe? Three times? I don't really know. I've lost track...." One of his four sons, Larry, gets on the phone to provide the correct answer. Once. After Frank's wife Margaret died in 1996, he had a girlfriend for about 10 years, until she passed away suddenly. Larry's now moved in to lend a hand, although these Coleman boys seemed to have figured out the secret of longevity on their own. Whatever it is.

"I've been asked that question many times, because I'm getting pretty close to the 100 mark," Frank says. It wasn't because he and his brother shared a common environment. They were separated during the Depression – Ernie raised by his mother and stepfather, Frank by his grandparents – before "he went his way and I went mine," Frank says. Eating right? "I don't think either one of us has been particularly careful about diet," Frank says.

Perhaps long life is in the genes? "Not really," Ernie says. "My grandmother was 99, and she was still keeping house. That's about it."

In the past decade Ernie's had a few lesions dug from his cheek, cysts pried from his shoulder, a chunk of his colon removed, two knee replacements, repairs on a broken femur and broken ribs and added a set of hearing aids. He was even hit by a train while vacationing in the Caribbean. True, it was one of those little tourist trains, more like a string of golf carts, but that'll still leave a bruise. Ernie's handled it all with such élan that a local rehabilitation center used his big, smiling face in a newspaper ad touting its services.

Ernie discusses these violations of his body in the same nuts-and-bolts manner as he does the repairs on a sailboat. The colon operation, for example. He spotted blood in a couple of bowel movements and subsequent tests detected cancer. Ernie explains how 14 inches of his colon were sawed away, then the two ends re-attached as easily as you'd fit together a pair of PVC pipes.

He has home remedies as well. It took four operations over a seven-month period to remove a cyst from his shoulder, and the usual gauze and tape couldn't stem the seepage from the wound. Ernie found that binding the area with sanitary napkins worked wonderfully.

Ernie sometimes sets himself up for these troubles. In the spring of 2003, the Rochester Yacht Club was burying a 65-foot-long plastic pipe across the harbor entrance, a rig designed to release a stream of bubbles to knock down silt before it flowed into the dock area. A crew of about 30 guys had assembled for the job, including a diver. Intent on taking photos, Ernie climbed a small hill overlooking the project. It was a cold day, and the ground had frozen into mud ruts. Ernie stumbled and fell. Someone called 911, and an ambulance carried him off to Rochester General Hospital. Diagnosis: Broken femur, five inches below his hip.

"They gave me pain pills, but I had a very rough night," he says. The doctors put him in traction. For the surgery he requested local anesthesia because, "I don't like to get knocked out.

"It didn't hurt," he says. "You feel the action." The splintered bone was wrapped in stainless steel wire to hold it together. Ernie'd seen guys in the service, wounded in action, bolted together in this manner.

Local anesthesia meant the surgeons had to follow not only their procedures, but Ernie's years of carpentry experience as well. " 'Make sure you get those legs the same length,' " he instructed. "The guy says, 'You think I'm some kid? I don't know how to use a ruler?' " Hammers were brought out to put in place the screws that would hold the metal rod in his leg to the broken bone. "You use a screwdriver for a screw," Ernie admonished the surgeon as he tapped away with a mallet. He did, once the screws were in place. The pins, Ernie learned, have threads only near the head.

More work would be needed on Ernie's undercarriage. The years had caught up to the cartilage in his knees. "My legs were so bowed, they looked like parentheses," he says. "I figured, what the heck, why don't I go for broke?" However, Ernie did express concern that knee replacements presented an engineering problem with his newly repaired femur. "Stainless steel rod meets a titanium knee," he says. "That's two incompatible metals." Ernie could solve this problem. " 'Put a piece of zinc between the two and you won't have that galvanic reaction,' " he helpfully suggested.

Fortunately, that's what replacement cartilage is for. No zinc for Ernie this time. He was laid up for two months, and came out with one leg straight, one bowed. It was another six months until doctors went after the next knee. While he was rehabbing from that realignment, and they had him sitting still, Ernie's cardiologist souped up his heart with a pacemaker. Incidents like his train trip into the Alps, and climbing that Mexican pyramid, had been the warning signs. "I figured I was stupid, taking two steps at a time," he says of the pyramid. "They told me, 'Your heart has a murmur in it. If it slows down and stops, it won't start up again.'"

Add it all up, and Ernie's been in the shop for the last decade. "I don't like it, I'm very unhappy about it," he says. "I'm older, but I'm not feeling that way. I'm unhappy I can't go to work on my knees."

As winter closes in on the 93-year-old sailor, he readies *Desire* for its winter hibernation, disconnecting the electricity, swapping out easily removable pins for the bolts that hold lines in place, until the mast is taken down for storage. Little things that will make pulling his boat from the water go easier and swifter.

But he can't get down on a boat's deck and work the wood fittings, sweating the details, as he once did. And on haul-out day, he'll see his role reduced in the haul-out crew from what he calls the "At Large," position – because it's getting difficult for him to clamber around the boats – to "Rover."

"Maybe I'll be transferring some dock lines," he says, accepting his fate. "But for the most part, I spend most of my time sitting on a chair."

He throws up his hands. "I'm older. So what? Live life like you can. Take life as it is. But don't leave it so."

Yet he cannot leave it so. One morning in 2004, Ernie was going down into basement workshop. He reached for a spot overhead that he always reached for when trying to keep his balance on the steps, and....

And, "I missed," he says. "I actually dove down the steps. I woke up and I thought, what the hell am I doing down here?"

Ernie struggled back upstairs and tried to wash the blood from his forehead, then sat down to recover. Someone came to the door. It was a yachting buddy who was supposed to meet Ernie at the docks so that he could borrow a buffer. When Ernie didn't show, he drove to Ernie's house. It's less than a five-minute ride. Ernie greeted him at the door, still bleeding. Over his protests, he was hustled into the friend's car, a sporty Corvette that felt every dip in the road, and sped to the hospital.

"Every bump we hit, it was, 'Man, oh man!' " Ernie grimaces, reaching for his side at the memory. "They were more concerned about my head than my ribs."

In fact he'd broken ribs 6, 7, 8 and 9. And it was painful. "You only breathe half a breath for several days," Ernie says.

This would be another extended period of healing. Except, this tumble brought about an unexpected result. Going in for the X-rays, "It'll take a couple of you to get me off this gurney," Ernie warned the hospital personnel who gathered around. He was mindful of the pain he'd been in for months, his inability to sit up once lying down, since that party game in Antigua when he'd wrecked his back.

Except now, "No pain," Ernie says, his eyes widening in wonder. The fall down the basement steps had completely eliminated the back problem. And it never returned.

"They couldn't make anything of it," Ernie says. "My doctor said, 'I wouldn't recommend that as a cure.' "

Chapter Fourteen

The folk singer Joan Baez had just been in town, which makes Ernie think of the 1960s, and the Vietnam War. "They really gave her trouble over that," he says of Baez's anti-war activism. But that was more than four decades ago, and things look a little different now. "I think we should have kept our noses out of it," he says. "She was right."

Ernie doesn't always speak properly – he sometimes calls the Pacific campaign of World War II "the Jap war" – but he's nevertheless a thoughtful man. "I think the U.S. is flexing its muscles too much," he says. "We've got one hell of a mess in Afghanistan and Iraq."

Ernie's sitting in his kitchen, on a beautiful fall morning in Rochester. At the end of his street, Lake Ontario is a steely, misty gray. Later in the week, Ernie will be taking *Desire* out of the water and putting it away for the winter. A sailing season is gone yet again, for the 38th time with *Desire*. It feels like a reflective morning....

Q: You've enjoyed a good, long, healthy life. How did that happen?

A: "I never worried about anything. I never was the kind of guy, when I had a headache, who took an aspirin. Now I'm pumping 15 pills a day. I've had a few tragedies, my wives dying. In my late 50s, I told myself, 'If I die tomorrow, I haven't missed anything.' "

Q: What's the most important thing you've ever done?

A: "When I married Evie, she had five kids, I had a little girl. Yeah, I would say that's the most important thing. I helped mold the kids. I feel the parent is responsible for a lot of the bad habits. Of course, you can't hit them anymore. I say, 'Spare the rod, spoil the child.' I never regretted a moment. Now my son Charlie says, 'If Dad's happy, that's all that matters.' Jan and Marilyn gang up on me." Ernie describes how, earlier in the summer, a growth had re-appeared on his left cheek. He put off taking care of the problem. Their insistence he see a doctor was simply nagging. But it was removed and, yes, it was cancerous. "They were asking me, 'Did you go see the dermatologist yet? Did you go see the dermatologist yet?' " Ernie waves his hand dismissively, and says of Jan, "You'd think she was my own child. She loves to sail. She loves to maintain a boat."

Q: Do you read much?

A: "No. I read magazines. Sailing magazines. I read them from stem to stern. I read short stories. I always take a book on trips." Ernie shuffles into the living room and returns with two John Grisham paperbacks, *The Last Juror* and *The Broker*. "I like the O'Brian books. I've read all 20 of them." That's Patrick O'Brian, author of a series of naval adventures set during the Napoleonic wars.

Q: So you do read?

A: "If I read for half an hour, I fall asleep."

Q: Ever been in a bar fight?

A: "No. Never. I've had a few fights, but not in bars. I almost killed a Marine once, then I got pulled off. I would have killed the son of a bitch." We can't let this story get away. While he was based in Maui, Ernie had been "palling around," as he calls it, with a member of the WAVES, or Women Accepted for Volunteer Emergency Service, the female division of the Navy. Ernie recalls one night trying to get into a dance, but he didn't have his ID card on him. It was, in fact, in his friend's purse, but that didn't make any difference to the Marine, who turned them away. In Ernie's estimation, the guy was being a jerk. The next day, Ernie and his WAVE pal were at the beach when, who should he spot in the water? His surly foil from the night before. Ernie swam up to him. "I could hold my breath for over a minute under water," he says. "I said to him, 'I remember you, you were the SOB who wouldn't let me in the dance the other night.' I stuck my head under the water and hit him in the gut with my head. That's one thing I eventually got over, when I got mad I would see red. I pulled him under the water. I would have drowned him, but a couple of my buddies ran into the water and pulled me off. The strangest thing is, I became good friends with him." That about-face came when Ernie drove a truck load of plywood up to Haleakala volcano, and the 4th Marine Division's camp, to use as flooring for the Marines' tents after the area's rainstorms. Ernie's antagonist was the sentry who waved Ernie and his truck through the gate. They recognized each other. Getting a man out of the mud heals a lot of wounds.

Q: Ever meet a celebrity?

A: "Ted Turner." That's when the TV mogul was at the Rochester Yacht Club in 1998 for The Ted Turner Great Eight Match Races. There have been other brushes with fame. "I saw Clark Gable in LA, almost a handshake away. I was very impressed with him. He was a man's man, a ladies' man. That voice of his was something else. Dorothy Lamour. I was really surprised at how small she was. She didn't have any makeup on, I hardly recognized her. It was a crowd situation. Makeup is a wonderful thing for women." He pauses for a half-second. "And men!"

Q: What's your all-time favorite movie?

A: "I think I was quite impressed with *Wings*. There were no women in it. It was strictly an airplane war." Ernie's taking about the 1927 silent film about World War I dogfights, although he's evidently forgotten that Clara Bow had a major role. Of course, he was a kid then, and his brain probably wasn't picking up on the romantic junk. Ernie was in high school when he saw the 1931 version of *Dracula*. "The one that scared me the most was that vampire movie. Bela Lugosi. I ran home in the middle of the street, I was so scared. And I lived a mile from the theater."

Q: What's the most beautiful place you've ever been?

A: "To me, I guess it's Lake Ontario. I've seen all of the shores of Lake Ontario, and I find a lot of beauty in that. I was very impressed with the Canadian Rockies, too. Marilyn did the driving, I just watched. They're so different than the American Rockies. Every turn we made was a different rock formation."

Q: What's it feel like to be at the helm of *Royal Clipper*?

A: "Dreams come true. The thrill of all thrills. Especially putting it through maneuvers. Tacking and jibing. Here I am in charge of this 5,000 tonnie."

Q: During the Cold War, did you think the Russians were going to drop an atomic bomb on us?

A: "No. No, no, no. I think they realized we had a few we could drop on them. I worry about Iran, the way they don't value life. They could drop some bombs on Israel, wipe them out. Then they get wiped out. But they don't care, they don't value life at all."

Q: What was your favorite car?

A: "The one I have now. It's a luxury car, it's got everything on it. It drives so beautiful. There's only one problem, it goes faster than it should. You can be doing 50 and you don't realize it. Eighty and you don't realize it." Apparently he's talking about the white 2000 Buick LeSabre parked in the driveway.

Q: How about something cooler?

A: "Hudson Terraplane, 1937 convertible. It had an electronic shift. It had this little thing on the wheel, and you pushed it, but it didn't shift until you put the clutch in." This little gadget was known as the "Electric Hand." "That was a fast car. We had drag races in East Rochester. I beat everybody because of that automatic shifter."

Q: You've played a lot of bridge. What's the secret?

A: "The secret is remembering what's been played. And also have a partner who understands the bidding. That's in, what do you call it? Duplicate bridge. I haven't played bridge in 13 years."

Q: You've said you were happy to break 100 playing golf. What have you learned from the game?

A: "It's good exercise. If I hit a bad shot I say, 'Oh, I've got another chance at it.' If I hit a good shot, 'Wow, I did that?' "

Q: What is your most unusual talent?

A: "Ambidextrous? I played tennis with no backhand, just shifting the racket. When I use a hammer, whichever hand picks it up does the work. Saw, same thing. Either hand. I write left-handed. Shoot pool, shuffle cards, left hand. Kick a football, right foot." This all came about after Ernie got his right hand caught in a door when he was 6 years old, nearly severing two fingers. "I couldn't use them when I was learning how to write, so the teacher had me write with my left hand. Until that, I was right-handed."

Q: What was your best year ever?

A: "Best year sailing? Golf? Bowling? One year I won everything with Roger and Diane." That's his two longtime crewmates on *Desire*, Roger and Diane Libby. Ernie wanders off into the hall and returns with a silver plate, first place in the under 30-foot class. It's from a Scotch Bonnet Race in 1994, sailing across Lake Ontario, rounding Scotch Bonnet Island, then back home. "That year I won the Freeman, which is a long-distance race. I won the fleet championship at the Rochester Yacht Club in my division. Fleet champion at Genesee Yacht Club in my division. The Oak Orchard Race, the Rochester race. I think it was seven first places, where I got yellow flags. Gold flags, they call them. The Freeman Cup was on a Wednesday. Sail to Sodus, then Ford Shoals, 10 miles east of Sodus. Round that mark, sail to Braddock Bay. Round that mark, sail to Rochester. A 40-mile spinnaker run. It was gorgeous."

Q: Do you think there is life on other planets?

A: "The latest news, it's possible. I think it's possible."

Q: Why do you like to dance?

A: "I love flowing with the music. Especially the waltzes. Fox trots. Rumbas. Salsas. I used to do them all. I loved to jitterbug. Evie and I used to cut some good rugs. She was a wonderful dancer. I did the cha-cha." Ernie begins to sing: "Tea for two, two for tea...."

Q: If you had never seen a sailboat, what do you think you would have done with your life?

A: "It's hard to imagine. Hard to imagine. In other words, I never gave it a thought."

Q: You always seem to know a lot about the things around you. The history, the geography, how stuff was made. How important is that?

A: "I have a very inquisitive mind. When I was a kid and I had toys, I used to take them apart and see what made them click. I always try to fix everything. I always like to know why and how."

Q: You've been involved in two wars, watched a few others. Is it worth it?

A: "You've got me wondering on that. In this Iraq thing, we didn't go far enough in the first place." He's talking about George H.W. Bush's 1991 Gulf War. "We should have completed that job. Bush got chicken on that. By the same token, I don't think Iraq will ever become one nation. It's been three nations forever. To combine three nations will not be easy. The Kurds have been the most successful, although they have a problem with Turkey. The Jap war, that was necessary, that was invasion, that's what brought America together again. Unfortunately, it didn't end wars, it wasn't the war to end all wars. There will always be war. In my lifetime, anyway."

Chapter Fifteen

Charlie Ross looks back on the twin calamites that preceded Ernie joining their family – his father Gilbert's suicide, the death of Ernie's second wife, Jen – and his judgment is unequivocal. "He saved our family."

Jan Ziobrowski remembers Ernie and Evie as something beautiful. "That's my favorite love story," she says. "I think everybody was happy about it. It's not like a marriage after a divorce. Both spouses were dead. They were married out of a common need. They needed a mom. We needed a dad. They grew to love each other."

Yet it isn't a fairy tale. Forging one family from two is a complex, difficult, ongoing process. The kids' ages ranged from married adult to rebellious teen to pre-schooler. Judy was already married and out of Evie's house. Shirley was 17, engaged and almost out: "My mother was against the marriage, let's put it that way," she says. Charlie was the teenager Ernie remembers as a difficult kid to talk to. John, just a little over a year behind, was taking his cues from Charlie.

And the two youngest, Jan and Patricia, were a mere 5 years old when Ernie and Evie married on April 7, 1961. "He took on a lot when he took on our family," Shirley says. And yet, "We just always thought he was amazing," Jan says. "Kind and stern at the same time. Stern, yet fair." Today, Jan is her stepfather's confidante on board *Desire*, keeping the crews intact for two nights of racing each week, keeping Ernie behind the tiller as he recovered from his decade of broken femurs and knee replacements.

A lot of healing has taken place. Bones and spirits. Even Evie's refusal to accept Shirley's husband eased with time. "It worked itself out," Shirley says.

Yet it hasn't worked out for the girl adopted by Ernie and Jen when she was two days old, Pat Coleman. She hasn't seen Ernie since his 80th birthday party. She is estranged from the family, trapped in Phoenix, living in a home for battered women, unemployed, utterly defeated.

"I should be where Jan is, Jan should be where I am," Pat says. On the phone, her voice sounds weak. She is not in good health. It's her heart, she says. "I would have, I should have been the one out there crewing on *Desire*." There is resentment, although little anger. As she tells her story, and it's a wreck of life, Pat knows what went wrong, but seems confused as to why. And yet, despite her dire situation, she clings to a sailing memory, and a long-distance phone call, in a manner that is at once both desperate and endearing.

How, given similar circumstances, does one kid take one road, while the other wanders off in a completely different direction?

At first, Ernie and Evie's union was the marriage of convenience as described by Jan. Evie's twin sister, Eileen, was Ernie's Madison Terrace neighbor. In fact, Ernie had built Eileen and Jake's house. "He was always a part of our life," Jan says. They'd socialized. Charlie even remembers being in Ernie and Jen's house when he was a little kid. When Ernie and Evie married, no introductions were necessary.

Early on, Ernie reached out to Evie's kids. "Before I even knew they were seeing each other, it was my birthday and the phone rang, and here's this guy singing 'Happy Birthday' to me," says Judy. The oldest of Evie's children, she was already married and out of the house. "We have the same birthday, Nov. 20. Every year, we call each other to sing 'Happy Birthday.' We try to beat each other, see who gets there first. He beat me this year."

They testify to the evolving relationships between Ernie and the kids, unaware that so many of their words echo each other.

Judy, the oldest: "Oh, my God, he's the greatest. Who comes into a family with four, five kids, and keeps their upbeat attitude? They all took to him as a father."

Shirley, second oldest: "He was a father figure for the boys and Jan. They were young when Dad died. It was his honesty. He was just a good guy."

Jan, the youngest: "Mom had been the disciplinarian. When Dad came in, the boys were teenagers."

Teenagers. And the young rebels would surely be testing the new guy.

Charlie, the oldest son: "He came in and instilled some discipline into my brother and I. We pretty much had the run of the roost."

With Ernie bringing in his carpenter's checks, and extra money repairing boats down at the yacht clubs, Evie no longer had to work. Adult supervision went up a few ticks. "That," Charlie says, "was a positive change in my life.

"I was a bit of a daredevil when I was younger. I would jump off the Elmgrove bridge into the canal. When Ernie heard I was starting to dive off the bridge, he came along and wanted to make sure I was doing it right." And Ernie didn't stand on the road shouting instructions, or show Charlie a Parks and Recreation Department film strip on canal safety. He showed Charlie how to do it by diving off the bridge and into the canal himself. "Because he had done it as a kid," Charlie says.

Such feats of physical flair are impressive when they're coming out of your elders. Charlie remembers being on construction sites on days when the kids were out of school, watching his ambidextrous stepfather's lunchtime carpentry challenges. "He could hammer nails with a hammer in each hand," Charlie says. "He'd say, 'Let's see if any of you guys can do this.' " Years later, Ernie underwent surgery for carpal tunnel syndrome. That's one procedure he forgets to mention while cataloging his replacement parts. Perhaps it's not as interesting as, say, bowel plumbing. Charlie says the doctor told him afterward, "Those are the hardest-working hands I've ever had to operate on."

Ernie came about them honestly. He and Evie were Great Depression kids, an experience that was always looking over their shoulders. "Dad more than Mom," Jan says. "He'd talk about things like how you could buy a loaf of bread for a nickel. But how a nickel was a lot of money."

It's that Greatest Generation ethos we've heard about. Work, Jan says, "is what keeps him going." She shakes her head grimly, the bearer of bad news. "Our generation will never make it. We just don't have the work ethic."

They also played hard. "They were a very socially active couple, Ernie and Evie," Charlie says. "They liked to have a few beers and play cards. They always had a lot of people around them. And they were very good dancers. People liked to watch them dance."

"He read us stories, drew us stick figures," Jan says. "They had dinner parties, clam bakes. He knows you have to grab the gusto when you can. Life is not a dress rehearsal.

"We could always come to him at any time and talk to him. If he didn't have the answers, he would help me find the answers. He helped me through divorce. A car accident."

Yet no one in the family had answers for their 60-year-old brother John in the summer of 2010. "He kept saying, 'I'm not dying, I'm just not feeling great,' " Jan says. Little wonder. "He had three kinds of cancer." John died that November.

No one wants to face death. Few people really want to think about it. Fewer still want to be around it. Ernie's most jarring experience with mortality, his final night on *Vincennes,* was not something he talked about. "No, never," Jan says.

"But we can't bury something that long and be rid if it."

No, never. You can't help but stumble across it. Ernie was the father that Jan remembered, and although Jan knew she'd had another father, she did not know the truth of it. "Not right away. I blocked it out," she says. The family protected the youngest daughter, did not speak of what had happened until she was 13. Even then, the details emerged by happenstance. Jan was babysitting for her sister Judy's children. "The kids knew and they said something about it," Jan says. Her father had shot himself in the woods behind the house. "I was always told," Jan says, "that he died in a hunting accident."

"It wasn't an easy time," Judy concedes. She was 18 when her father died. "Unfortunately, everybody just didn't talk about it. It's one of those things that should have been met head-on."

The unhealthy silence that served as both protection and denial from Gilbert Ross' death was not an option with Evie. By 1995, it was clear to all that her health was failing. There was no evading the issue; it had to be met head-on. Ernie did the best he could to ease her way. "The last day, he called us and said she was going really fast, you need to get down here," Charlie remembers. "That was the only time I ever saw him get mad at her. Well, mad isn't the right word. She wasn't speaking, her breathing was very shallow. Ernie went for a short walk down the street, and that's when she died. He came back and we told him. He just kind of shouted, 'You had to leave me when I wasn't here!' "

It wasn't anger. "He was a wonderful caretaker, a loving man," Charlie says. "They were a couple in love. It was an inspiration to watch them."

"I used to watch them walking down the street holding hands," Jan says. "Making sure nobody moved Dad's puddle."

Now he was alone again. Just Ernie and his puddle, the lake. Evie's kids watched over him as best they could. But they were spread all over the country. John was in Florida. Judy and her husband Frank Farrand were retired and living on Oneida Lake, 1½ hours away. Shirley and her husband Elvin – he passed away a few years ago, having long ago won Evie's approval – were 1½ hours away in the other direction, in Horseheads, near Elmira. Pat had gone into exile in Phoenix. Only Jan, Charlie and his wife Betsey remained in Rochester.

"He was miserable," Jan says. "Lonely. He pretty much shut down. We'd do dinner once in a while. But we were all dealing and hurting on our own. We didn't go out of our way like we should have. Mom was the glue that kept the family intact."

And then, Marilyn? "That was a bit of a shock for us," Charlie says. "But it's worked out for Ernie. He's gotten to see the world."

"He asked us, 'Would you rather I sit home alone? Again?' " Jan says. "But traveling, with him and Marilyn, that's been a lifesaver. We all think it's been a great opportunity."

Marilyn's daughter, Julie Lockner, was all for it. She was 25 years old at the time, married to a guy 11 years older than she is. "I thought it was a riot," she says. "He looked like – what's the name of the guy on the cover of the frozen seafood packages?" A handful of marketing-department creations fit that description, Mrs. Paul excluded.

Julie's brother, Steve Lockner, is another late-life addition to Ernie's family tree. He's a bit of a twisted limb, he admits, a garrulous fellow who compares his rough-hewn manner to the Randy Quaid character in the *National Lampoon Family Vacation* films. "I'm the old man with a sailor's mouth who rides a Harley," he says. But he feels a kinship with Ernie as an ex-military man – Steve was a Marine – and as a man who's rebuilt his life as well. Steve's divorced, and lost contact with his first two children. He's since remarried, acquiring two more kids the second time around. Both of them have already done time as Marines. Like Ernie, Steve's a hands-on guy, a mechanic living in the rural outpost of Byron.

"He's a old-school guy, know what I mean?" Steve says. "You can tell a veteran, he has an old-school way of doing things. He doesn't worry about, 'Oh, no, I've got to give the kids a time out.' He's a proud man, and I'm proud to be his stepson."

Steve shares his stepsister Jan's bleak view of the future. "You kind of wish kids nowadays knew half as much as he does about the world," he says. "Then you wouldn't worry about them. But, they're lazy.

"Ernie has outlived, what, three wives now? The old guy doesn't stop. And he still has a passion for sailing, even after what happened to him on the *Vincennes*."

It's a steely resilience, tempered over nine decades of life. A fourth marriage? Just when his journey drifts to a stop in the water, Ernie seems to catch sail-filling breezes. Perhaps it has some connection with what he's learned on the lake, and what Jan says is the best piece of advice that he's shared with her. "Always know where the wind is."

The wind carried Pat elsewhere. Everyone seems to hold their breath for a moment when Pat's name comes up.

"You know that Reba McEntire song, 'The Greatest Man I Never Knew?' " Pat says. "That speaks volumes."

The one that goes, "every day we said hello, but never touched at all."

Ernie and Jan call her Trish. Others in the family call her Patti. Patricia is fine, she says. Or better yet, Pat. She doesn't know who she is, or where she's going. Once she starts, the story pours out like water from a breached levee. "I was in an abusive relationship, and I didn't even know it," Pat says. "We had no friends. She was an alcoholic, and she knew how to push my buttons."

Pat explains that she is gay. For a man of Ernie's generation, that can be particularly vexing. What does his life experience tell him about this one?

Pat continues. "We were living at a motel, and after 18 months we got evicted. So then we're living out of her truck, and I heard about it every day. She was going to get me evicted from her truck. One day we were arguing more than usual. She punched me in the face, broke my glasses."

Pauline, her partner, then drove away in her pickup truck, leaving Pat standing in a parking lot. The two dogs, a Pekinese and a chow, went with Pauline. It's the last time Pat saw any of them. "I had those dogs since they were puppies," Pat says wistfully. "One was 9 and one was 10."

"Since then I've lived in three domestic violence shelters. Now I'm in a transition shelter, for people over 50. It's supposed to teach you how to be self reliant.

"At least," she says sardonically, "they don't have all these screaming kids around."

That was a year ago. Where and when did this start?

"Jan was the apple of my mother's eye, she could do no wrong, I could do no right," Pat says. Yet that resentment was erased, she insists, looking back to the day she was 18 or 19 years old. Evie fell off a bicycle and broke an ankle, "and I moved in with her. We were best friends all of a sudden. It turned out she was the most accepting one about me being gay. I think she got to see a side of me she wouldn't have seen otherwise."

Shortly afterward, Pat went off to nursing school. She became an emergency-room nurse in Rochester, then in Buffalo for 12 years. Ernie and Evie, she says, visited her only twice. "I'm 90 miles away and nobody comes to see me," Pat says. "I might as well be 3,000 miles away."

Perhaps Pat's world was one that Ernie wasn't comfortable with. She and Pauline moved to Phoenix. That's not 3,000 miles, but 1,900 can feel like enough. Twenty years later, distance hadn't fixed anything. In fact, it got worse. Pat lost her job in 2009. "I had some problems with the head of nursing," she says. "I surrendered my nursing license voluntarily. A patient accused me of stealing two soda pops from a room. Then the focus became the suicide attempt.

"I tried to kill myself, a year ago in October. I felt I was totally alone, I didn't have a job, money." She argued with Pauline. "I said, 'I could walk out this door and kill myself, and you wouldn't care,' and she said, 'No.' So I took a bunch of pills. Went to a secluded spot, took the pills and waited for death. I ended up throwing up, massive diarrhea. I made it out to the street and someone with a phone called 911. I was in the hospital a week or 10 days, urgent care center.

"Then I went back to the motel."

Pat says she's been born again for years. It doesn't seem to have had the advertised effect. "I've repented and been baptized. I'm a Christian. I liked the Lutheran church. I tried Pentecostal for a while. That's 10 times worse than Baptist.

"I don't think loving somebody is a sin. I've got Jesus and the Lord to help me."

The conversation has returned to Pauline.

"I call her Satan. She worked in a floral shop. I got her the job, I saw the 'help wanted' sign in the window and said, 'Why don't you try that place?' Her life was one beer after another, like a chain smoker. When one was empty, she'd go get another one. Twelve, 14 beers a day. I sure don't miss that 'pop-pop' when you open it. And she would make it louder just because she knew it bugged me.

"I know it will sound pretty sick, but, one of the reasons we stayed together, the dogs were so attached to her...."

A sudden blackness surges through Pat. "If I had a gun, I'd direct it at my nursing supervisor, my roommate and then myself."

Seconds later, the darkness passes.

"I'm working on a new career," Pat says. "I was a nurse for 32 years. I'm excited about this." She's taking classes to learn billing, so she can work in a medical office. Pat's having heart problems – "I had to quit half the medication I was on because I couldn't afford it" – and she figures office work would be less of a toll on her body than the nursing. "Standing 8½ hours every day, there's no way I could do that. I'm not even 56 years old, and I'm falling apart."

She pauses. "If I had it all over again," she says wistfully, "I would have done things differently."

Differently, starting with life in Rochester.

"When I flew back for my mother's funeral, Dad and I – I think it was the only time – we went out on the boat alone, by ourselves," she says. "It's like, when you do meditation at the center here, and they tell you, 'Pick one thing that was your happiest moment.' That sail with him, that meant a lot. We were talking about stuff like, he wanted to donate his body to science. I said, 'Wouldn't it be better to be cremated and throw your ashes out on the lake?'

"I had been home a couple of weeks before that, to visit my mother before she died. He drove me to the airport, and he was saying, 'When she gets better, we're going to do this, we're going to do that.' And I said, 'Dad, it's too late!' I don't know how much time he thought she had.

"I can't afford to come back," Pat says, now worried about how much time her father has. "I'm just afraid I'm not going to see him again alive."

She resented the attention that Ernie and Evie lavished on other people, and their frequent socializing. "It was all about cocktail hours, nightcaps, the morning eye-opener," Pat says. What Jan calls a "typical sibling rivalry" is something that Pat insists runs much deeper.

Yet for years, Jan had been the only family member with whom Pat communicated.

Then, after having not spoken to her father in more than a decade, in December of 2010 Pat expressed a holiday wish to Jan. "I told Jan, the one thing I want for Christmas," she says. " 'I want Dad to call me.' He did. We didn't get into anything really heavy. But, it was like those 10 years never happened."

And here, the story departs from the Reba McEntire song.

"The first couple of times he called, he missed me. He left a message. He said that he loved me.

"If we never talk again, I saved the message. So I can play it back whenever I want to."

Chapter Sixteen

Ernie was in the right place at the right time: Eyes wide open, the 20th century.

Things were happening right in front of him, even if he didn't know it. Like the day some guys down at the docks offered Ernie and a couple of his teenage buddies a ride out into Lake Ontario on their big motor launch. This was the early 1930s, the country was sagging beneath the Great Depression, and this kind of offer didn't come by often. They rode out to the middle of the lake, where the launch met another boat. The two crews quickly transferred a big load of boxes, wrapped in bulky sacks, onto the boat Ernie and his pals were riding. Then they returned to shore, the men on the launch encouraging Ernie and his friends to wave as they passed the Coast Guard station at the mouth of the Genesee River, before puttering past it and tying up at the docks. Nothing to see here, just a little joyride. As Ernie walked away, he saw the mysterious sacks being discreetly loaded onto a waiting truck.

"They told me to not say anything about it," Ernie says. "So I didn't." Decades later, Ernie figured it out. It had been Prohibition time. The launch owners were bootleggers. Ernie and the boys had helped provide cover for a shipment of illegal booze from Canada.

That's pretty typical of Ernie. Every day with him, another story emerges. "Didn't I tell you that one?" he says in amazement.

No. What else have we missed?

Now Ernie's riding shotgun as he conducts a leisurely driving tour of his life. This will take all afternoon. No matter. "I don't keep track of time anymore," he says. The tour starts in East Rochester, along Commercial Street, through the heart of downtown. After the death of his father, George Coleman, Ernie moved here to an apartment with his mother and her new husband, Alfred Kyle. It was on Commercial Street that Ernie – he must have been 5 or 6 at the time – stopped an electric trolley car by standing on the tracks and, with a handful of pennies, demanded that he be taken to visit his grandmother.

Turn right on Grant Street. The streets are that very American thing of being named after presidents or trees. The house Ernie grew up in looks very different from when he lived there. It's a typical small, two-story home of the era. The front porch has been enclosed since he moved away, like a hand held over the eyes, no longer a space in which to hang out on a summer day and shout out to neighbors passing by. "I used to like to sit there and watch the storms come in from the west," Ernie says. "That two-car garage back there, I helped build that. I built my first boat in there."

His stepfather, a lightweight Navy boxing champ, taught Ernie how to fight in that backyard. The two were close, and Ernie respected his toughness. Alfred was a Navy fireman, stoking the ship's boilers. "As a fireman, you had to be rugged," Ernie says. That toughness extended to family matters, and a house full of Kyle boys. "They fought among each other when they were growing up," Ernie says. "But if you messed with one of them, they stuck together. They had a lot of respect in this town."

Grant Street was Ernie's home through his high-school years, then during his mother's illness and death from cancer. He brought his first wife, Ruth, to live here before moving on to Marion Street. Alfred, with the Grant Street house to himself, remarried. "He couldn't stand being alone," Ernie says, an echo of his own words following the deaths of his second and third wives. Ernie's mother is buried in the Coleman family plot, in a cemetery not far from the Grant Street home. Alongside her first husband. Alfred is in another cemetery, buried next to his second wife.

Ernie will allow for no such confusion when he goes. "I'm gonna be powder off the side of the boat," he says. "Three buddies are there already."

That was Pat's suggestion, wasn't it?

On the way out of East Rochester, Ernie points out the high school, built on the site of the old school he once attended. The middle school is next door. "They put in a pool," he says, nodding at the outdoor addition. "Our pool was Irondequoit Creek."

It's a 10-minute ride to Rochester, and the house on Marion Street. Another two-story residence, it's no longer the duplex shared by Ernie and his brother Frank and their wives. "That lot goes way back," Ernie says, pointing around the side of the house. "We had a Victory Garden out back. That garage is new. And the house had two doors in front, one to the upstairs apartment, one downstairs. Wow, it is different."

Gleason Works, the gear-manufacturing plant at which Ernie worked, is nearby. The neighborhood's built up now with the detritus of fast-food commerce: a KFC, a Tim Hortons. "America is different than Europe," Ernie says. "They don't tear things down in Europe." He points to a tall, battered old roof, crowded out of the picture by newer buildings in front of it. "They made ammunition there during World War I," he says. Artillery shells.

That building appears empty. Gleason Works is still active, and while the mission has not changed, the gears it is grinding are no longer for cannons and tanks, but trucks. But there's not as much call for precision American gears these days. A section of the building has been rented to the George Eastman House, a film and photography museum, as a vault to store items of historical value in a cool, dry environment.

By the time he'd left Gleason Works, joined the Navy and returned in one piece, Ernie's idea of what he'd do with his life was evolving. His passion was building things – the cottage on Canandaigua Lake, the garage on Grant Street, his first boat, coffins for Navy fliers who'd misjudged the distance to a mountain. He sits in the parking lot at Gleason Works as workers begin leaving for the day. Ernie recalls how, after returning from the war in 1945, he'd turned his back on such hot, indoor shift work in favor of working outdoors, in construction. And repairing boats at the yacht clubs.

Ernie preferred being his own man, but temptations came his way. A salesman from 3M, the chemical company, brought Ernie a compound that had been used to seal wood joints on aircraft carrier decks in the sweltering South Pacific, suggesting he try it on the yachts he was refitting. Ernie used the goop on seven boats, and both he and 3M were satisfied. "They offered me $10,000 a year, plus expenses and commissions, to sell the stuff," Ernie says. Pretty good money in that day. "I would have been going up and down the coast, as weather permits, and demonstrated this stuff.

"I turned it down."

On to the first home he owned, on Titus Avenue in the suburb of Irondequoit. Ernie lived here with Ruth. It is immaculate, well landscaped. "Boy, did they change it," he says, impressed. "I planted those trees, by the way," he adds, pointing out two hefty cedars in the front yard. The house has acquired an addition, the second floor now extending over the garage roof. "I built my last boat in that garage, right under those bay windows," he says. Ernie was sailing with the Newport Yacht Club on Irondequoit Bay at the time, and he was the toast of the coast. Those regattas often ended at his driveway. "My house looked like a flophouse," he says. "Everybody brought sleeping bags and just threw them on the floor. We had so much damn fun."

But things change, as Ernie keeps saying throughout the drive. While Lake Ontario was once visible from the front yard of this house, it's now obscured by tall trees. And his marriage was crumbling. By 1950, he'd told Ruth he wanted a divorce. He left her with everything, except his tools, his clothes and his last Snipe, *Feather*. The Navy summoned Ernie again, he remarried, Ruth remarried, she died after falling down the stairs in this house. Several families have probably since passed through here; as the car pulls away, the front door opens and an African-American teenager steps outside.

Across the river and into the western suburb of Greece. Ernie has never been to CM Gifts and Militaria. Perhaps this visit will pry loose something new from Ernie. A tiny store specializing in combat-ready M-16 bayonets, division coffee mugs, canteens, gas masks and $121 sand-colored desert boots built to specs by the U.S. Army's official supplier. History is here. One wall is decorated with newspaper stories, obituaries, photos and certificates honoring Medal of Honor winners with local connections. On one crowded wall is an old newspaper photo of a ship that looks quite similar to *Vincennes*. It is *Philadelphia*, from the class of cruisers built after *Vincennes*.

The store's owner, Charles Rabidoux, has been around all kinds of veterans. The ones who talk. The ones who don't. He sometimes offers them advice on how to go about collecting benefits, or whom to see about medical or psychological issues. Rabidoux has a calm, encouraging manner about him.

Ernie putters around. "This is interesting," he says quietly, the well-stocked shelves a wave of distant memories, before being directed to a glass case filled with medals, mostly brass, affixed to bright ribbons. The military-industrial complex, and assorted manufacturers of reproductions, produce an astounding number of tchotchkes. Rabidoux patiently explains what some of them represent. A medal for those who completed training in the United States and were subsequently sent overseas. A medal celebrating the World War II victory. Here, one awarded to anyone who served in the South Pacific naval campaign.

Ernie nods. "I had some of these, but I didn't hang onto them," he says. He points to another medal, one with a purple ribbon and a heart shape enclosing a bronze portrait of George Washington. "Of course, I had one of those."

The Purple Heart. For servicemen wounded in action. Ernie had never mentioned it.

The driving tour of Ernie's life moves on toward the lake, and a mere three weeks of his life. A period after he'd quit Gleason Works, but before he joined the Navy. The Odenbach shipbuilding plant is a massive shed, visible from a long distance over the treetops. Ernie was a machinist here, when Odenbach was building 180-foot-long, shallow-draft oil tankers, called lighters. Alongside the building sits Round Pond, which received the finished ships. "We'd stand over there and watch them plop into the water," Ernie says. "One every eight days." The new ships would be floated along Round Pond and an accompanying channel until they came to Edgemere Drive, which runs parallel to the beach. The channel cut through the road, flowing beneath a bridge. When a tanker with its 30-foot beam had to pass through, pontoons below the bridge were filled with air, raising the bridge and allowing it to be pushed out of the way. The ship continued on into Lake Ontario, up the St. Lawrence River, to the Atlantic Ocean, and to the war.

Odenbach was tough work, tough on a man's health. Ernie recalls how the building would fill with smoke from welding equipment. But now the building's silent, a fragile cavern of iron ribs, sheet metal and broken glass, like an impossibly big and abandoned cicada shell lying in a meadow, surrounded by well-rutted gravel parking lots. "It's amazing it's stood this long," Ernie says.

The tour resumes, following the lake toward the Rochester Yacht Club. Past the closed and soon-to-be-razed Russell power station, with its twin smoke stacks, each 250 feet tall. Seen from out in the lake, they were the most prominent aspect of the shoreline. Ernie undoubtedly won many races by checking these stacks, the drift of the smoke informing him of the wind direction. The builder of this now 63-year-old relic, Ernie says, was also a sailor who insisted that the stacks line up precisely north-south, so that boats could check their compasses against them.

Ernie knows this kind of stuff. Not too many people do. Today, sailors use a Global Positioning System. Some of what Ernie has learned over the years may seem quaint, like how he repairs the rust holes on his old van by covering them with sheet metal held in place by pop rivets. But it works.

At the lake, his natural habitat, Ernie settles in at the Rochester Yacht Club bar and orders a glass of merlot. "This is my project every year," he says, running his hands along the shiny, mahogany-red wood, heavily varnished. "I've got 14 coats on it now." The clubhouse itself is a comfortable elegance, although Ernie laments that this wood is only a thin veneer, so he has to be careful as he sands it for the next year's coat, lest he grind through to the rougher wood below.

Perched on his stool like a hobbit, he chats with the female bartenders. They know him. Everyone seems to know Ernie, although he insists he's not in here often. But he understands this environment. "I cut my teeth on the yacht clubs of the '30s," he says. Back then, he helped build the Newport Yacht Club. Build, literally. The club had 18 members, and each sacrificed a week's pay to buy the materials. "I was making $15 a week," Ernie says, so it was no palace. "We built it, did the painting, searched for the materials. We made a club out of it." The Genesee Yacht

Club – he belongs to it now as well at the Rochester Yacht Club – is of the same rec-room environment.

A few stray thoughts, and the glass of wine, catch up with Ernie after nine months of ruminating on his life. He's been to seven funerals this year, with another on the schedule. The subject of his daughter Pat – the one in so much trouble in Arizona – comes up. "She was always getting involved with losers," he says sadly. "There's nothing I can do." He dwells on this family of eight children that he acquired. "Heartaches and headaches, but I loved it with a passion," Ernie says. It's a series of complex relationships amplified by his own long life. His oldest daughter, Judy, is three years older than his wife, Marilyn.

Ernie looks out the big windows, to the far side of the river, and sees the terminal where a few years ago the city's fast ferry would tie up. Ferries had been a part of Ernie's Rochester throughout his early years. For his Senior Class Day, 75 of his fellow classmates at East Rochester High School rode the street car into Rochester, all of the way up Lake Avenue, where they caught the ferry across the lake to Cobourg. Leaving at 7 in the morning, they were home by midnight. "It only cost me $3.25," Ernie says.

Seventy years later, the new fast ferry debuted in 2004, a part of the declining city's hopes for revival. It would now cost $37, one way, for a trip to Toronto. It was a beautiful ship, but financially unworkable, and was out of business after two summers. Three years later it was sold to a German company, and today churns its way through the channel between Spain and Morocco.

Ernie had never bothered to ride it. "Now, it's so easy to get to Toronto by car," he says. "And it's quicker, really." Speed and convenience have overtaken the more-measured ways of his youth.

As Ernie nurses his glass of wine, he dwells on more change. He was once fascinated by flying. He remembers as a kid seeing a Curtiss Jenny biplane, built 70-some miles away in nearby Hammondsport, rumbling low over East Rochester. He chased it down the streets and through the fields to the now-extinct Brizee Field – Jennys could fly remarkably slow – to watch it land. This was the beginning of Ernie's youthful dalliance with flight. "All I knew was the Wright Brothers before that," he says. "I was going to be a pilot, no question." Airplanes were still an uncertain commercial enterprise then, mainly working as mail planes, generally seen as more of an adventurous amusement than something that could change the world. "Then they built 'em big enough to carry passengers," Ernie says. "But they thought jet planes wouldn't make it. All of a sudden they realized, you get there quicker, and carry more people."

Ernie's remembrances often have a beautiful naïveté. Dashing through meadows as a kid while a Jenny soars overhead. Back then, the pilot would take you up for $1 a ride. Entrepreneurs that they were, Ernie and his buddies worked a deal where they'd wash the planes for a free flight. Forget jumping off the canal locks. Flying was the new frontier, the new thrill. Seeing the massive dirigibles of the day – *Hindenburg*, *Shenandoah* and *Macon* – silently passing over Rochester during his youth further stoked that interest.

But Ernie's romanticism has always been balanced by reality. *Hindenburg*, *Shenandoah* and *Macon* all came to newspaper-headline endings. His romance with the air, and perhaps the securing of his partnership with the water, cooled at Brizee as well with one more landing, if it can be called that. "He was coming in. He didn't make it," Ernie recalls. The plane wrecked in a creek bed.

"They go 'splat' when they hit," Ernie says. "I didn't see the crash, but I saw them taking out the body. Looked like a bowl of jelly. I didn't go back there. That turned me off."

Chapter Seventeen

A muggy and extraordinarily dark evening smothered the southwestern Pacific Solomons. No moon illuminated the waters around Guadalcanal Island and its accompanying string of islands, including Florida and Tulagi, with its golf course and cricket club built by the British as a way of dragging Western civilization to this part of the world.

And, just to the north of Guadalcanal, Savo Island.

For two days, *Vincennes* and its sister ships, *Astoria* and *Quincy*, and the Australian cruiser *Canberra*, had been covering the landings of the Marines on Guadalcanal and Tulagi. Lobbing 8- and 5-inch shells at the islands and swatting at the Japanese fighter planes, dive bombers and torpedo bombers arriving to challenge the invaders. The Imperial Japanese Navy, despite reports of its presence in the area, had yet to make an appearance.

On this, the evening of Aug. 8, 1942, combined fleet commander Rear Admiral Victor Crutchley had a handful of warships at his disposal. Six heavy cruisers, two light cruisers, 15 destroyers and five minesweepers. Crutchley divided this force in half. One group to watch the southern approach to the islands, the second group to patrol the north.

The plan did not work. Incredibly, seven Japanese cruisers and one destroyer entered New Georgia Sound under cover of darkness virtually undetected, the few warnings of their presence ignored. In a short, brutal battle that lasted little more than 30 minutes, four Allied cruisers sailed into the fog of war. For weeks, it was as though they had never existed.

In Ernie's home city of Rochester, for four cents a day – and as best as the wartime censors would allow – the *Democrat and Chronicle* slowly, ever so slowly, broke the news to the folks back home. The war, heavily edited, unfolded in thick, black headlines such as these:

BATTLE STILL RAGES IN SOLOMONS

"Jap Resistance is Considerable, Navy Discloses," the subhead announced on Aug. 10 in the first of The Associated Press stories from the scene:

"Competent British circles dismissed the Japanese claim of sinking or damaging 28 vessels in the Solomon Islands battle yesterday and suggested that the enemy, as in the past, was making sweeping victory assertions to prepare the Japanese people for bad news of their own losses.

"Flamboyant Japanese broadcasts that 11 transports and 17 other 'Anglo-American' warships were damaged suggested that the great naval battle was covering an invasion to drive the enemy from the southern Solomons, 900 miles northeast of Australia."

On the following day, "Disclosing this late yesterday afternoon," the AP reported, "the Navy revealed that the furious assault, in which the Marines were strongly backed by warships and planes, had already cost the United States forces at least one cruiser sunk and two damaged and two destroyers and one transport also damaged.

"The Japanese, whose counterattack was launched 'with rapidity and vigor,' have suffered a 'large number' of surface units destroyed and put out of action, the Navy statement said.

"The Navy statement warned that 'considerable losses' must be expected."

Two days later, "details of the naval battle are 'not yet available,' " the *Democrat and Chronicle* told its readers. And other fights demanded attention. The Japanese were in Alaska's Aleutian Islands and were invading New Guinea.

Meanwhile, in Europe:

GERMANS SMASH NEARER TO STALINGRAD

A curiosity from newspapers of the day was the practice of running delayed dispatches, reporters' stories often held up for weeks until approved by the wartime censors. On an inside page of the Aug. 17 *Democrat and Chronicle* was one such story that, despite the absence of details such as ship names and locations, appears to have been filed from *Vincennes*' squadron after it left Pearl Harbor.

"This American naval force, bound for 'somewhere,' gave an impressive preview of things to come today in a slashing, thunderous drill with live ammunition which was marked by the fine timing of a crack football team.

"Orange flames spurted from the muzzles, which were enveloped in thick shrouds of coal-black smoke seconds later as the guns settled back into their sockets. Huge white puffs rose from the tiny uninhabited island where the projectiles crashed and exploded.

"It was all over in what seemed like a few minutes...."

A sentence that eerily foreshadowed the battle that was to come.

Ten days after *Vincennes* and its fellow cruisers had engaged the Japanese at Savo Island, the news reports recycled U.S. Navy claims:

NAVY CLAIMS SEA VICTORY OFF ISLAND

A secondary headline carried the caveat "Spokesman Warns Victory Cost U.S. Losses." As the story noted, "The Navy carefully refrained from announcing the extent of damage to American forces, saying that such information would be of value to the enemy – but it had previously announced that one U.S. cruiser had been sunk and two cruisers, two destroyers and one transport damaged."

Truth closed in two days later, in an official statement from Australia. "Prime minister John Curtain today announced the loss of the Australian cruiser *Canberra* in the Solomon Islands battle." The statement promised "few casualties." Small comfort to the families of the 84 men who died on that ship.

By Aug. 21, news reports announced, the U.S. Marines were "mopping up" on Guadalcanal, and a day later the big black headlines announced:

JAP FORCE IN SOLOMONS WIPED OUT

It was almost too easy to believe. News reports on Aug. 23 informed readers back home in Rochester that "Marines Force Japs To Pay At

27-To-1 Ratio In Solomons." Official word from the front arrived via one of the delayed dispatches, where a reporter returning from the battle reported all was well, with no mention of the early morning hours of Aug. 9 off Savo Island.

Stalingrad was still front-page news. The battles raged on in New Guinea and the Aleutian Islands. And battles raged in courtrooms as well. Comedian Georgie Jessel's wife had been granted a divorce after two years of marriage. She had been only 16 when they'd married, but she now realized that the 44-year-old Jessel was "too old for me and I am too young for him."

And there was this to worry about now:

ROMMEL ATTACK IN EGYPT DESERT

On Sept. 4, the newspaper's front page featured a large photo of a returning U.S. Navy warrior, accompanied by a few sentences summarizing his estimate of the Guadalcanal campaign action. "First Lieutenant-Commander George Huff, first Navy man to arrive on the mainland from the Solomons since American occupation, is pictured in San Fran yesterday. He told how Australian flyers carried empty bottles with them, which they tossed out of their planes following the bombing of Tulagi. The bottles 'whistled all the way down,' scaring the natives and the Japanese invaders, Huff said at press conference."

Bottles, flung as a prank. Not a word on his fellow U.S. Navy men on *Vincennes*, *Quincy* and *Astoria*. The photo was accompanied by this disturbing headline:

MARINES FIGHT OFF NEW JAP LANDING

No, the Marines were far from mopping up. Meanwhile, help was on the way. A photo inside the Sept. 6 edition showed Clark Gable, having enlisted in the United States Army Air Force, and now in officer candidate school at Miami Beach, getting his rifle inspected.

On Sept. 11, the sinking or damaging of three Japanese destroyers by U.S. Navy planes in the Solomons area was reported. Two days later, a headline over another story claimed:

U.S. UNITS BAG 96 JAP PLANES AT SOLOMONS

Below it, another headline, "Battleship, cruiser hit in record air victory." While the details were a bit off, both of these delayed reports were apparently from The Battle of the Eastern Solomons, which had indeed cost the Japanese a large number of aircraft, a light carrier and a destroyer.

Each day's news revealed a new success, and more reason for the folks back home to scour vacant lots for the scrap-metal drive, another frequent front-page concern. But the news was often delivered with admonitions. A story headlined "Report on Nazi Convoy Battle" tells of word coming from the Atlantic of German submarines converging on Allied ships, with a small box inserted within the story:

"Warning – this news comes from an enemy source. Bear in mind there is likelihood it was designed for propaganda purposes."

Inside the section, the publisher of the *Democrat and Chronicle,* Frank Gannett, was one of the featured speakers at a forum called "News, Censorship and Morale." Gannett was quoted extensively, including his comment, "The American people have shown that they can stand bad news. The disaster at Pearl Harbor, the beating that Gen. Stillwell admitted he took in Burma and the loss of the Philippines did not destroy our morale."

The Sept. 6 headline "Allies Admit U-Pac Attack" confirmed the bad news that had been reported by the "enemy source" a few days earlier. Although, it hedged, the claims that 19 ships were sunk are "nowhere near the truth and bloated to the bursting point."

The next day, this big headline:

CARRIER YORKTOWN SUNK AT MIDWAY, NAVY REVEALS

This was Sept. 17. *Yorktown* had been lost on June 7.

The next day, somewhere between the harrowing headline proclaiming Stalingrad's fate hanging in the balance and an advertisement cautioning, "Look out for wartime constipation," came another delayed report:

"The 1,500-ton destroyer *Jarvis*, with possibly 172 men aboard, has vanished in the southwest Pacific and is assumed to have been sunk by Japanese submarines or aircraft, the Navy announced yesterday, and the speedy auxiliary transport *Little* also has been lost.

"Their destruction raised announced U.S. naval losses in that conflict to five ships sunk and five damaged, as against at least 22 Japanese vessels sunk or damaged.

"Previously it had been revealed the destroyer *Blue*, the auxiliary transport *Calhoun* and an unidentified cruiser had been sunk in the Solomons and two cruisers, two destroyers and one transport damaged."

Jarvis' newspaper obituary appeared five weeks after it had actually been sunk. Heavily damaged while protecting the transports during the Guadalcanal landings, the destroyer had limped away for repairs, narrowly missing the Japanese fleet as it arrived at Savo Island. With its radios disabled, *Jarvis* was unable to transmit a warning, and continued on. But thinking it was a cruiser that had escaped the slaughter in the early morning hours of Aug. 9, the Japanese sent 31 airplanes after the ship and sank it with the loss of its entire crew of 233 men.

According to that news report's scorecard, U.S. Navy losses to that point in the war were 43 ships sunk or scuttled, 12 damaged. Japanese ship losses were estimated at 400 lost or damaged.

On Sept. 29, readers learned, "Smashing with terrific force at the Japanese in both the Solomon and Aleutian islands, Army-Navy-Marine corps airmen in the last five days have destroyed at least 49 enemy planes and damaged five ships, one of which probably sank, without the loss of a single American plane in combat."

Just a few pages from this triumphant report was more discussion on wartime censorship. Byron Price, the government's director of censorship, told yet another gathering of publishers that while their newspapers had done well in not publishing information that might be of value to the enemy, they "have done a poor job of informing the people why some of the information has to be withheld."

If newspapers weren't publishing information that would be of value to the enemy, they were also publishing fiction that was of little value to the people. Often the information that the American public received arrived piecemeal and out of context. "U.S. Reveals Japs Sank Two Transports," the *Democrat and Chronicle* told its readers on Oct. 1, the news still trailing real time in the Solomons. "Small Losses in Pacific Attacks Reported." These were *George F. Elliott,* an aging passenger liner converted into a troop ship, which had been set afire when a Japanese torpedo plane crashed into it during the same battle in which *Jarvis* was initially damaged, and *Gregory,* a World War I destroyer converted into a transport. *Gregory* had been lost on the morning of Sept. 5 near Savo Island, in the same battle with three Japanese destroyers that claimed *Little.* Despite the picture that was being presented to readers of a Solomons Islands campaign in which the Japanese forces were being "wiped out," the Japanese were actually very much still in the battle.

And then, the slap of a rolled-up newspaper landing on the front porch on the morning of Oct. 13 announced to Rochester and the world what had happened to Ernie and his shipmates:

3 BIG CRUISERS LOST, NAVY REVEALS

After more than two months of drifting first in the water off of Savo Island, and then through the bureaucracy of the Office of Censorship, the newspaper reports were startlingly frank. "Heavy Loss of Life Reported From Naval Action," read one headline. "Survivor Reveals Sharks Periled Wounded Men," another reported breathlessly.

A sailor from *Astoria,* a Texan named Lynn Hager, was interviewed. "We'd been fighting constantly since the beginning of the Tulagi battle, 36 hours before," he said. "We expected a Jap naval force the next morning and we needed rest."

It is Hager who reveals in the story that ships were machine-gunning sharks in an attempt to keep them off the survivors struggling in the water.

But it was not long before the home front had reason to celebrate once again. On the very next morning, the *Democrat and Chronicle* greeted its readers with:

U.S. FLEET SINKS SIX JAP WARSHIPS

"Thus did Uncle Sam's Bluejackets and aircraft avenge the loss of the cruisers *Quincy, Vincennes* and *Astoria,* which were sunk Aug. 9 during the initial phase of the American offensive against the Solomons," The Associated Press reported. "Thirty minutes after the first gun was fired, the battered Jap force was in retreat."

Some wartime license was in effect here. This was what was later to be called the Battle of Cape Esperance, the third of the five big naval battles that were a part of the Guadalcanal campaign. It was indeed a U.S. victory, although the Japanese losses were one cruiser and three destroyers sunk, a second cruiser heavily damaged. American losses were one destroyer sunk, one cruiser and one destroyer heavily damaged. And while two of the Japanese ships were sunk by marauding American aircraft after the action had been broken off, one aspect of the news report was dead on. As had been the case in the loss of the four Allied cruisers two months earlier, the actual battle of the Battle of Cape Esperance lasted only 30 minutes. It was an echo, once again, of the delayed dispatch filed from the doomed U.S. squadron "bound for 'somewhere,' " and its training exercise. "It was all over in what seemed like a few minutes...."

All it took now was a few minutes. The best of naval design had been easily eclipsed by the technology to destroy these ships.

Chapter Eighteen

The Erie Canal is history that wound through the geography of Ernie's early years. He conquered it on his epic canoe trip in 1931, swam in it during the summers, and learned how to dive off the gates of Pittsford's Lock 32 on the New York State Barge Canal, as it had been known since 1918, which gave boats a 25-foot boost to the next level, on the way to Buffalo. "I was 14, 15 years old at the time, and I remember watching a girl diving from the top of it," Ernie declares. "I said, 'Well, if a girl can do it, I can do it.' "

He could. Ernie was developing into a strong swimmer. He remembers summers at his parents' summer home in Crystal Beach on Canandaigua Lake, when he'd slip into the water and swim to the far shore, "a good two miles away," he says. "I was a stupid kid. I'd catch hell from my parents for that."

But then he'd go and do it again.

In the midst of the winter of 1933-34, when Ernie was 17, more adventure came calling again from the direction of the canal. "The only time in my lifetime they didn't drain it," he says. The Three Musketeers couldn't let this opportunity slide by. They plotted out a skating trip, starting from Lock 32. Destination Newark, nearly 29 miles away.

At first, "I skated a little farther along than the other two guys," Ernie says. "I always try to be first in everything, I guess." The ice on the canal was about four inches thick, good enough to keep everyone moving along. Except where someone had cut a large fishing hole. Ice had just started to form over the spot when Ernie slid to a stop right over it, looking back to check on the progress of his companions. Then he disappeared from sight.

"I'm in the water, it's like the lights are turned off," he says. "I'm looking up. 'Where is that hole?' I saw something that looked like a 25-watt bulb. 'That must be it.' "

Ernie pushed himself up from the bottom, 12 feet below the ice. He swam toward the light, and it grew larger and larger until he emerged from the water. "By that time, the guys were there to help me out," he says.

They gathered brush and built a fire on the shore. "Fortunately, one of the guys smoked, so we had matches," Ernie says. "They kept changing clothes with me. But basically, I stood and froze while my clothes were drying."

And then the boys continued with the trip. "We were only four miles into it," Ernie says with a shrug. They skated on to Newark, and then back.

He could have died in that water. "One of my nine lives," Ernie likes to joke. Another life could have been used up after falling down the basement stairs at his Madison Terrace home. Ernie's first wife, Ruth, died in a fall down the stairs at her home. Or colon cancer could have gotten him. It is the third-most common cancer afflicting Americans.

You have to wonder what role that winter morning on the canal, when Ernie fell through the ice and instinctively fought for survival, played in the early morning hours of Aug. 9, 1942, when he escaped from a flaming warship as it slipped beneath the water, an ocean and a continent distant from the waters where he'd learned to sail and swim and dive. Experience, plus a dose of good fortune, that perhaps allowed Ernie to survive, while 332 of his shipmates did not.

Ernie had thought he could talk about that war experience now, 66 years later. But the nightmares were only slightly below the surface. He talks about his divorce, the death of two of his wives. He talks with unnerving frankness, humor even, about the series of surgeries that he's endured over the past decade. He talks about his joining the Navy, the training, the days leading up to his departure from Pearl Harbor, and the 22 months he spent afterward on Maui. But when it comes to the Battle of Savo Island, he backs off. The nightmares return. He is hearing the screams of his fellow sailors in the water.

Vincennes during maneuvers off Hawaii in June 1942, shortly after Ernie had joined the ship. One month later, *Vincennes* would be lost in the Battle of Savo Island.

Aging veterans speak of similar experiences every evening on The History Channel. They have described these events to writers. Some of the vets break down in tears after all these years. Others choose simply to not talk about their experiences, except in the most veiled of ways. That's Ernie. His family knew he was a World War II Navy man, but until recently did not know that he was on a ship that was sunk in battle. Most of them do not know the name of the ship. *Vincennes.*

We have already said this much: A muggy and extraordinarily dark evening smothered the southwestern Pacific Solomon Islands on Aug 9, 1942. No moon illuminated the waters around Guadalcanal Island and its accompanying string of islands, including Florida and Tulagi, with its golf course and cricket club built by the British as a way of dragging Western civilization to this part of the world. And, just to the north of Guadalcanal, Savo Island....

But much of what we know, and thought we knew, of what the naval historian Samuel Eliot Morison describes in *The Two-Ocean War* as "probably the worst defeat ever inflicted on the United States Navy in a fair fight" remained a secret from the American public for months afterward. Some facts were obscured for decades. Misconceptions and deceptions live to this day.

As *Vincennes* charted a course that would end abruptly off Savo Island, the attitude of the day – often a mocking dismissal of the Imperial Japanese Navy and its ships – did little to prepare the Allies for the battles ahead. In *Fighting Fleets,* an overview of the world's navies of the day, author Critchell Rimington writes, "Japanese cruisers are known to be compact and highly efficient fighting machines, even though their uneven decks and pagoda-like conning towers have been the cause of much naval amusement." This was a book published in 1943, with the outcome of the Pacific war very much in doubt. Near the back of *Fighting Fleets,* in an addenda labeled "Naval War Losses," is a list of warship losses by nation. These ships of the Imperial Japanese Navy, "the cause of much naval amusement," had already done their dark work. Turning to the final pages of *Fighting Fleets,* we see that *Vincennes, Astoria* and *Quincy* had already taken their places under the heading for U.S. losses.

This dismissive attitude extended into the highest ranks of the Allied command. In their 1992 book *Disaster in the Pacific: New Light on the Battle of Savo Island,* writers Denis and Peggy Warner, with Sadao Seno, pointed out that the commander of land-based air forces in the southwest Pacific, Lieutenant General George C. Kenney, embraced clichés that were racist, and a dangerous underestimation of their Japanese opponents. "Too much of their population," Kenney said, "is peasant class – rice planters, fishermen, rickshaw pullers – who are too dumb, too slow-moving and utterly lacking in mechanical knowledge and adaptability." And this was in September 1944, after *Vincennes, Astoria* and *Quincy* had been joined on the *Fighting Fleets* addenda by many, many more U.S. ships.

Disaster in the Pacific reveals more errors in Allied judgment as the two fleets closed for battle. "Neither the *Vincennes* nor the *Quincy*, which had only recently arrived from the Atlantic, had held night battle exercises or night target practice for at least 15 months," the Warners write. Most of the Allied commanders believed that a night action between warships was unlikely. Yet, the Warners point out, "hard training and night fighting were the twin pillars of naval preparation" for the Japanese navy. And had been since 1904, when Japanese destroyers surprised the Russian navy at Port Arthur, initiating the Russo-Japanese War. Since then, the Warners write, surprise "had been the key element in Japanese military thinking."

American preparations for the coming Guadalcanal invasion had not gone well, despite the assembling of a vast task force of U.S. and Australian ships. The war correspondent reporting back by delayed dispatch to the readers of the *Democrat and Chronicle* had adoringly described the "impressive preview of things to come today in a slashing, thunderous drill with live ammunition which was marked by the fine timing of a crack football team." But in reality, the dress rehearsal for the landings at the Fiji Islands was a failure. The landing craft couldn't get ashore because of dangerous reefs, and the exercise was reduced to the cruisers lobbing their 8-inch, 335-pound shells at the island, while airplanes practiced strafing runs on beach crabs.

Yet the landings on Guadalcanal and Tulagi on Aug. 7 went as smoothly as anyone in the Allied command dared hope. The ships had closed in on the islands at night, under cloud cover. *Vincennes* was among the big ships firing at hoped-for Japanese targets in the darkness, the shells red arcs in the night sky. As dawn arrived, the Marines' landing on Guadalcanal was startlingly unopposed, the Japanese having withdrawn into the jungle. It was a tough fight on Tulagi before the Americans gained control.

And then, the combatants for the Battle of Savo Island assembled for their fight.

The U.S. and Japanese navies entered the war with 18 cruisers apiece, children of the 1922 Washington Naval Treaty. With Europe in ruins after World War I, the thinking was: The next war won't be so bad if there were fewer and smaller guns. The treaty limited cruisers to 10,000 tons displacement and no armaments larger than 8-inch guns. Japanese cruisers built in the '30s tended to creep over 10,000 tons in violation of the treaty, but most analysts rate the fleets as pretty even. The major difference in the two navies' cruisers was in torpedo tubes. The U.S. cruisers went without, while the Japanese cruisers were armed with torpedoes that far outperformed any other navy's version of the weapon.

Yet ships that carried Ernie and his crewmates into battle were rapidly becoming an anachronism, anyway. The naval thinkers were now concluding that surface gun battles between large ships were in their twilight. In fact, four American cruisers launched just before the attack on Pearl Harbor, the *Atlanta* class, represented an abrupt change in U.S. naval strategy. These ships were armed with torpedo tubes, as though the cruisers were expected to engage in the same close-range exchanges with an enemy as destroyers had done. These new ships had depth charges as well, replicating a destroyer's anti-submarine duties. But most importantly, the main turrets were now fixed with smaller 5-inch cannon, along with a host of smaller guns, all faster-firing guns more suitable for anti-aircraft defense than the 8-inch cannon of the last decade's heavy cruisers. The *Atlanta* class also eliminated the scout planes that cruisers typically carried, planes that were to play a key role in the Battle of Savo Island, even though they never left their ships. Cruiser-based scout aircraft would be superfluous in the radar-enhanced navies of the future. With the increasing emphasis on the construction of aircraft carriers, plenty of planes would be at hand. Navy thinkers were anticipating the cruiser's role evolving into carrier escorts invited to the vast Pacific dance.

Neither the commanders of the U.S. fleet patrolling off Savo Island nor the equipment they had on hand had caught up to the strategies emerging from the drafting boards. Indeed, two days after the landings on Guadalcanal and Tulagi, the Navy pulled from the battle its three aircraft carriers, fearful of losing them. Naval battles in the first six months of the war had cost it two carriers, *Lexington* and *Yorktown*. So the air was under the control of whatever aircraft were based on the bomb-cratered air strip that the Marines had captured at Guadalcanal, and what the Japanese could bring with them to the fight. As they had just lost four aircraft carriers at the Battle of Midway, it wouldn't be enough to affect the battle.

Curiously missing from this fight was Task Force 1, the American Pacific fleet of battleships that included three pulled from the shallow mud bottom of Pearl Harbor and, in the eight months since the attack, had been thoroughly modernized: *Maryland, Pennsylvania* and *Tennessee.* But with German U-boats terrorizing the convoys of the Atlantic, oil transports were being diverted from the Pacific. Moving fuel around the Pacific was a logistical nightmare. And the seven battleships of Task Force 1 were the Navy version of the 1957 Cadillac Brougham: gas hogs.

Also curiously missing from the Battle of Savo Island was the commander of the landing force cruiser screen, Rear Admiral Victor Crutchley, a British Royal Navy veteran of the World War I Battle of Jutland. On Aug. 8, hours before the battle that night and early the next morning, he took the cruiser *Australia* out of the southern group of patrolling cruisers so that he could meet with the commander of the Guadalcanal landings, without telling his ship captains what he was up to, or who was in charge.

All of this worked against the Allied fleet as Japanese Vice Admiral Gunichi Mikawa's seven cruisers and one destroyer, each flying a 23-foot long white pennant so that they could more easily identify their comrades in the battle, rushed under cover of darkness from the north through New Georgia Sound – or "The Slot" as it was called by the Allies. Each card played seemed to fall the way of the Japanese, whose ships were hidden on the edge of a storm squall, lightning occasionally flickering through the dark clouds, as they fortuitously passed unseen between two U.S. destroyers to reach the rest of the Allied fleet. Blunder after blunder was committed by the doomed Allies, who had split their forces, misread their radars, dismissed Japanese scout planes and ships as their own, erred on the positions of their own ships and, as Japanese shells first began hitting the Australian cruiser *Canberra* at 1:43 a.m., mistook the explosions as the actions of the Marines fighting the Japanese on the islands.

From the opening seconds, the battle was illuminated by flares dropped from Japanese floatplanes, star shells fired by the U.S. cruiser *Chicago*, and then flames from the *Canberra*, which was out of the fight just two minutes after it had begun, struck by as many as 30 shells before it could even train its guns on the enemy. Then *Chicago*, after a brief exchange with the Japanese squadron, inexplicably charged off in the wrong direction and out of the battle.

Just as the U.S. Navy had been taken by surprise at Pearl Harbor, and as the Japanese had been taken by surprise by the Allied landings in the Solomons two days earlier, now the Allies had been taken by surprise by the Imperial Japanese Navy. Having scattered the southern group of Allied ships in mere minutes, the Japanese circled south of Savo Island, a small volcanic peak jutting up in the middle of The Slot. They were heading east and then north, toward the northern group seven miles away led by *Vincennes*, which was unaware of – as James D. Hornfischer writes in his 2011 book, *Neptune's Inferno: The U.S. Navy at Guadalcanal* – "the spectacular catastrophe of the preceding four hundred seconds."

Mikawa was astonishingly gracious when he wrote afterward about what was to take place now. "The element of surprise worked to our advantage and enabled us to destroy every target taken under fire. I was greatly impressed, however, by the courageous action of the northern group of U.S. cruisers. They fought heroically despite heavy damage sustained before they were ready for battle. Had they had even a few minutes' warning of our approach, the results of the action would have been different."

In fact, the Allies had been warned. An Australian Lockheed Hudson bomber spotted the Japanese fleet on the afternoon before the battle. Morison's history of this moment carries the day; he wrote of how the plane had not broken radio silence, but merely returned to its base and – the story taking on outlandish embellishments with time – the crew dawdled over tea before reporting their sighting.

Disaster in the Pacific, using testimony from the day and a report that wasn't declassified until 1973, exonerates that air crew. Who knows why – perhaps a search for a scapegoat – but for decades the Navy and Morison's version prevailed. We now know otherwise. The Allied high command was aware that the Japanese were within striking distance. Commanders and captains were notified. But proper preparations were not made.

And the obvious was ignored even as the first of the Allied ships lit up the night sky in flames. "WARNING – WARNING – STRANGE SHIPS ENTERING HARBOR" the U.S. destroyer *Patterson* radioed. The message never reached the bridge of *Vincennes*, leading the northern group. Instead, a message on yet another course change was delivered. The message did reach the bridge of *Astoria*, but no one thought to relay it to gunnery, in preparation for battle. *Quincy* never heard the message at all.

Inexplicably, uncertainty followed what should have been a very clear next message: *Astoria*, *Quincy* and *Vincennes* were suddenly illuminated by spotlights from the Japanese ships, at 7,500, 9,500 and 10,500 yards respectively, in a misting rain and light breezes. *Vincennes* Captain Frederick Riefkohl ordered a radio message be sent to whatever fellow ship that was to turn off the lights. An eruption of water just in front of Riefkohl's ship moments later, at 1:55 a.m., announced the arrival of Japanese shells. The Americans could even see them, black shapes in the night sky, yet with an orange glow.

Confusion reigned – were those our ships? – even as the shells began striking *Vincennes*, first hitting the carpenter shop, the bridge, the hangar and the communications antennae. The hanger was particularly problematic. Although the fuel had been drained from the five aircraft carried by *Astoria* and *Vincennes*, the SOC Seagull float planes on all three ships nevertheless went up in flames, providing the Japanese gunners with carnival shooting-gallery targets, while also allowing the Japanese to turn off their own lights and fire from the protection of darkness.

Minutes into the battle, Riefkohl seemed to believe that his ship might still be the victim of friendly fire, sending blinker signals and hoisting signal flags. The captain of *Astoria* thought this might be the case as well. Still the shells and torpedoes came, as the Japanese ships separated into two lines with the three American cruisers in the middle, delivering death from both sides.

Official Battle Damage reports can be a breathtaking mix of analytical and brutal reading, the conclusions as clinical as an autopsy. In the case of *Vincennes*, *Quincy* and *Astoria*, the autopsy was issued on Sept. 3, 1943, more than a year after the battle.

The shell hits sustained by the ships are frequently numbered in the report. Of *Vincennes*, the investigators write, "The carpenter shop just aft of the hangar was hit three or four times (Hits Nos. 52, 53, and 54) and fires were started in this compartment." The destruction reached deep into the ship, to the boiler rooms: "The No. 1 fireroom is believed to have been hit by either a projectile or torpedo as there were no surviving personnel from this space...." "The intensely hot fragments from a High Explosive projectile inside a ship have few if any equals in setting fires within confined spaces...." "Topside personnel accounted for the majority of the casualties...." "At least 57 hits were received in the spaces discussed above. Undoubtedly, as in *Quincy*, there were many other hits in these and surrounding spaces which were not reported."

There were far too many holes to be plugged by mattresses backed with 2x4s. The Japanese could hardly believe their good fortune, as "every salvo caused another enemy ship to burst into flames," one Japanese veteran of the battle later wrote. "For incredible minutes the turrets of enemy ships remained in their trained-in, secured positions, and we stood amazed. Yet thankful while they did not bear on us. Strings of machine-gun tracers wafted back and forth between the enemy and ourselves, but such minor counter-efforts merely made a colorful spectacle, and gave us no concern." One dramatic photo taken from a Japanese cruiser shows *Quincy* illuminated by Japanese spotlights and enveloped in brightly lit billowing smoke. Off to starboard is a ball of flame searing the night sky. That is *Vincennes.*

The Official Battle Report continues: "In all three ships these fires were fed by topside paint, life jackets, signal flags, airplanes, airplane spare tails, wings, parachutes, ships' boats, lubricating oil and kerosene, which made the area between the bridge and the after bulkhead of the hangar an inferno beyond human endurance."

Aboard *Vincennes,* this area included the carpenter shop, Ernie's station, and its stores of highly flammable materials. Flames licked up the paint that Ernie and his mates in the carpenter shop had covered the ship with as it churned across the Pacific. More hits knocked out the range finders, gun-control electronics, the secondary 5-inch guns and inter-ship radio, and firefighting became impossible with the water mains broken. Steering control from the bridge was lost. The damage report tells of an 8-inch shell – hit No. 7 – penetrating the second turret but not exploding, instead setting fire to exposed powder. These fighting ships, designed to deal damage to their enemies, were proving deadly to their own crews. "Attention is invited to paragraphs 25 and 45," write the authors of the Official Battle Report, "in which the 5"/25 caliber ready-service ammunition exploded as a result of projectile hits.... When so ignited, cartridge cases may be expected to jump out by rocket action in a flaming condition, and to burn on deck or to roast other charges so that they too ignite in succession."

Vincennes, its guns manned by incinerated corpses, was doomed. Two torpedoes from the Japanese cruiser *Chokai* may have struck it in the port side, although the reports are never in total agreement, so furious was the assault. Flaming wreckage and live shells were dumped overboard, and the gun turrets were now running on auxiliary diesel generators, or were being cranked by hand. The ship was a tangle of smoke, steam and dead sailors. The decks were slippery with blood. Below decks, breathable air was becoming difficult to find. Yet *Vincennes* still managed to hit the Japanese cruiser *Kinugasa* with a round of 8-inch shells. But in the 20-minute fight, it managed only two full salvos from its nine 8-inch guns, and another two six-gun salvoes.

"What a scene!" wrote *Life* magazine photographer Ralph Morse. He had been taking pictures of the combat on Guadalcanal and had locked his precious negatives in a safe aboard *Vincennes* when he learned it would be heading stateside for overhaul after this action. He lost everything except his life. "The sky was lit up with shelling and fires on ships," Morse wrote. "Ships were shelling ships and ships were sinking all around us. I kept shooting like mad. Sailors were being hit all around us, and sailors were being killed just next to me."

What a scene, indeed. As Hornfischer writes so pointedly in *Neptune's Inferno*, "It was about 2:40 in the morning when Admiral Crutchley, from the bridge of the *Australia*, observed a trio of objects burning on the sea between Savo and Florida islands and wondered what calamity he had missed."

Word from Captain Riefkohl was passed around to abandon ship shortly after an apparent third torpedo hit by the light cruiser *Yubari* set *Vincennes* on a shuddering, lurching list to port. The wounded were helped into life jackets. Life rafts that weren't burned were heaved over the side, and lines were draped over the side of the ship for men to climb down into the sea as others held flashlights. Some men simply jumped into the water. *Vincennes* continued to heel to port, its entire superstructure aflame and beginning to crumble. It was probably the first and only time that any man on board had witnessed the astonishing sight of steel burning. The *Vincennes'* propellers emerged from the water, a Sword of Damocles waving over the men already in the sea, struggling to cling to floating debris. The ship slipped lower into the water and began to capsize and now its crew, including Riefkohl, could simply step into the Georgia Sound. *Vincennes* continued to roll until its mast smacked the water, almost hitting Riefkohl, its decks a flaming mass of scout planes and broken teak wood, the smoke stacks dipping into the water until the ship turned turtle and went down by the bow.

Just as the war correspondent had written of the Allied dress rehearsal at the Fiji Islands, "It was over in what seemed like a few minutes." Twenty-two, in fact. At 2:15 a.m., the Japanese ships had ceased firing and withdrew back up the sound. *Quincy* and *Vincennes* went down within 15 minutes of each other, *Quincy* first about 2:35 a.m. Both ships filled the warm, shark-infested sea with more than 1,000 oil-covered sailors, many wounded or in shock, clinging to mattresses and shell casings and rafts and furniture and lumber, worried as well that they might get run over by a ship in the dark confusion. The sailors drifted for six and seven hours, in some cases longer, before the destroyers *Ellet* and *Wilson* came to the rescue of most of *Quincy*'s men. The bulk of the crew of *Vincennes*, which sank more than a mile away from *Quincy*, was scooped up by the destroyers *Mugford* and *Helm*. Morse, the *Life* photographer, was in the water for eight hours. "Luckily, it was a very noisy battle with shells going off and torpedoes hitting ships," he wrote. "I guess any shark in his right mind got the hell out of there."

Large and small acts of heroism continued through the night. Men on the surviving ships dove into the water to rescue the shipwrecked. *Astoria* and *Canberra* survived into the next day before sinking, *Canberra* scuttled by American torpedoes.

It was the first of seven major naval actions in the waters surrounding Guadalcanal. The Japanese had fired 1,844 shells of various caliber, reporting 159 definite hits and another 64 probables. And the hits were effective, the shells timed to explode not on contact, but after penetrating deep inside the target. Of the nine 8-inch gun turrets on the three American cruisers, six were destroyed by direct hits. The American ships got off 471 shots, recording 10 hits. Allied losses on the four sunken cruisers, the damaged ships, and on the destroyer *Jarvis* when it was set upon and sunk afterward, were 1,275 men killed, more than 700 wounded. Japanese losses were about 50 men killed, perhaps twice that many wounded.

The area became known as Iron Bottom Sound for the number of warships that came to rest on the sea bed. *Vincennes, Quincy, Astoria* and *Canberra* were merely among the first. By the end of the battles, each side had contributed 24 large ships to the graveyard and lost nearly the same number of aircraft each, 450. As many as 5,000 American sailors died, and 4,000 Japanese, during the Guadalcanal campaign, which labored on until the Japanese finally withdrew in February 1943. As for the U.S. Marines and Army troops who stormed ashore, the official death count is 1,592. For the Japanese defenders, about 20,800 dead.

Those are the numbers. Here's another number: 500 fathoms. That is about the depth at which Robert Ballard found two of the lost cruisers from the Battle of Savo Island more than a half-century later.

Ballard is the celebrity oceanographer best known for leading the expedition that discovered the ruins of *Titanic* on the floor of the Atlantic Ocean in 1985, at the tail end of an expedition secretly financed by the U.S. Navy to find two submarines it had lost in the 1960s, *Thresher* and *Scorpion*. He has since used submersibles and remote-controlled vehicles to explore other wrecks as well, all with their own violent histories; the German battleship *Bismarck* in 1989, the torpedoed ocean liner *Lusitania* in 1993, *Yorktown* in 1998, even President John F. Kennedy's *PT-109* in 2002 (they found a torpedo tube). Film crews accompany Ballard, converting this gruesome archaeology – remember, people died here – into entertainment delivered directly to you and your family in your living room.

And this may be acceptable, so long as we learn the lessons of history.

The lessons of history? Ballard spent three weeks at Iron Bottom Sound in 1992, after a mostly unsuccessful '91 expedition, and this time quickly uncovered the *Canberra*, and then the *Quincy*. His expedition discovered 13 wrecks in all from the Guadalcanal campaign's naval actions, although *Vincennes* was not one of them. The resulting documentary and lavishly illustrated book detailing their finds, *Robert Ballard's Guadalcanal*, show the Japanese battleship *Kirishima*, lying upside-down, its guns and command centers smashed into the mud, a huge anchor chain wrapped around one propeller like a leash entangling a dog. Of *Canberra*, we see a starboard anchor, still attached to the hull, and a forward turret with its 8-inch guns. Of *Quincy*, the bridge, looking remarkably intact despite having taken a hit that killed nearly everyone there, including the ship's captain. The ships are covered in marine growth, and are generally so battered that American, Japanese and Australian wreckage lose all nationality. The photos' greenish tint reveals the destroyer *Monssen*'s torpedo tubes and a hole in the hull of the Japanese destroyer *Ayanami* where a wheel that was used to aim the torpedoes can be seen. And unidentifiable broken steel, remnants from a ship only recently designed as the future of naval warfare, *Atlanta*. It was destroyed during the night battle of Nov. 12-13 off Guadalcanal, its useless state-of-the-art design sunk not only by Japanese shells and torpedoes, but by U.S. shells accidentally fired at it in the confusion. And there is 100 feet of the destroyer *Barton*'s bow, the section where the ship broke in half lost in the darkness.

The darkness. In truth, without intense lights illuminating only short spans of this mess, a diver would never know that most of this was sitting on the mud floor of Iron Bottom Sound, the steel slowly and quietly giving way to the salt water. Photographs present only quick shards of the damage suffered by these ships, not only during the battle, but during their difficult freefall to the ocean floor. So as is frequently the case with Ballard's expeditions, the renowned marine painter Ken Marschall has been brought in to give us the full picture of what these war relics look like today. *Canberra*'s big guns, never used in this battle, point crazily, as do *Quincy*'s. At *Quincy*'s two forward turrets the guns are aimed upward, as though this game fighter had been firing at its enemies even as it dropped out of sight. Its bow is ripped off and completely missing just before the first turret, the stern and aft deck is collapsed and bent upward.

In the deep, eerie blue light that Marschall gives each scene, the ships look like toys at the bottom of an aquarium.

It is an elegant, ugly futility. In the final pages of *The Winds of War*, Navy Commander Pug Henry is standing on an overlook in the early morning darkness, looking down on the wrecked battleships after the attack on Pearl Harbor. "He could almost picture God the Father looking down with sad wonder at this mischief," Herman Wouk writes. "In a world so rich and lovely, could his children find nothing better to do than to dig iron from the ground and work it into vast grotesque engines for blowing each other up?"

History predicts that will never be the case for mankind in general. But sailing Lake Ontario for all of these decades, Ernie Coleman has done so. He has found something better to do.

Chapter Nineteen

Charlie Ross came to suspect over the years that a few pieces were missing from Ernie's story.

"He never talked about the war at all, Charlie says. "It was 2008 before I ever got anything out of him. All he ever told us is he was stationed in Hawaii. He was up at our house for Thanksgiving, and I just asked him, 'What else did you do in the war? You must have done something else.' "

Ernie's response was perhaps inadvertently prescient: "What, are you writing a book?"

"I just told him, 'Well, you're getting up there....' " Charlie pressed him a little more. "I knew he was in the Navy. I asked him, 'Were you on a ship?'

"He said, 'I have nightmares when I talk about it.' "

More than 60 years later, and still *Vincennes* haunted him. Yet the nightmares hadn't chased Ernie from the water. That final night on *Vincennes* was something for the most part that Ernie, Charlie says, "had put somewhere else." A distant compartment where it wouldn't be heard from as he moved on with his life.

Ernie has continued to sail and win races, undeterred by the vastness of a lake that stretches across the horizons in much the same manner as the South Pacific, paying no mind to low-lying clouds or distant shores that can look like warships, if you allow the mind to take you there. Or the rumble of thunder from an approaching storm, so much like gunfire.

True, Ernie was beached for a few years, after marrying Evie. He'd sold his third, carefully crafted Snipe and moved into her home, miles from the lake. Responsibility called for more time with his newly acquired family.

And Ernie's ideas of raising a family fell in line with his own personal philosophy: Keep busy. Looking to put some focus into the two oldest boys, he brought home a junk 1952 Plymouth. Junk to most people. A seemingly useless carcass, but a learning experience for Ernie's two newly acquired teenage sons to pick over. "There were a few hundred acres of field out back, toward the railroad tracks," Charlie says. "It was for us to learn how to take apart and put back together, learn about engines, and to drive around in the field. He always thought it's useful to have a skill like that."

Yet during that decade, Ernie also slowly drifted back toward the prevailing winds of Lake Ontario. He was determined to take a couple of the kids with him. Evie, too, if the winds were really working in his favor. In much the same way that he had dragged home the near-comatose Plymouth, Ernie returned one day from a remodeling job having partially settled the bill by taking off the hands of a customer a homemade plywood sailboat, stored in the garage and painted what Jan remembers as "state park green."

"That's what he started to teach us to sail on," Jan says. "We used to carry the mast home, and he locked up the boat with a chain on the beach. Then someone stole it."

Perhaps it was for the best. "It leaked a little bit," she says. And soon enough, while on another job, Ernie had spotted yet another sailboat languishing in a garage. Once again, he made it a part of the deal when the work was done. This was a Sunfish, a one-person sailboat. But Ernie piled on board with his two youngest girls, Jan and Pat. That's how they began sailing the regattas. Ernie and a boatload of girls.

The sailors in the family turned out to be Jan, Pat and Charlie. And later, after he married Marilyn, her daughter Julie. "Julie took to it," Jan says. "She was a natural at it. I'm good at it because I love it. She's good at it because she's a natural. Tricia and Julie, they can put the math-science thing behind it. I just wing it."

Charlie got to the game late, and not because of any direct influence from his stepdad. "I didn't know anything about his sailing as a kid," Charlie says. Already a teenager when Ernie arrived, he was going his own way, eventually finding the path to a 38-year career at Eastman Kodak.

But by the mid-'70s, he was spending time on friends' boats. Sailing was a social thing. Steer in a circle a few miles out from port, "have a cocktail, that sort of thing," Charlie says. Before long, he was racing on a friend's veteran Soling, a 27-foot racing boat, a design known for competing in the Olympics. This one had lost its Olympian edge a bit. "I kept asking, 'Why isn't this boat competitive?' " Charlie says. "And my friend says, 'It's old.' "

So they split the cost on a newer Soling, and Charlie announced to Ernie that he was planning on joining the Rochester Yacht Club. Coincidentally, Ernie had been scraping up the cash to sign on with its next-door neighbor, the Genesee Yacht Club.

By then, Erie had returned to sailing in a serious way, buying *Desire.* Charlie remembers Ernie proudly showing off the new boat by taking a few family members out to get a close look at Turtle Rock, a large, flat obstruction 200 feet or so off Lake Ontario Beach. It generally lies just below the surface of the lake, but peeks out a bit when the water level is low, usually in the fall. In one of Ernie's rare moments of sailing misjudgment, he ran *Desire* right over the top of Turtle Rock and got stuck. "The Coast Guard had to send a boat over to get us off," Charlie says. "They had to fire a line over to us, because they couldn't get any closer. I always like to remind him of that."

Turtle Rock was a lesson learned the hard way. Other lessons arrived in a less-jarring manner.

"I don't know if instinct is the right word," Charlie says of what he's seen of Ernie's sailing style over the years. "His senses are very acute to wind speed and wind changes. He can feel it on his face, on the back of his neck, on his nose."

"He's so in tune with it, sometimes he gets a little intense," Jan says. Particularly moments like the start of the race, what Ernie calls, " 'threading the needle,' when he gets to the starting line and ducks between these big boats, and you think there's no way he's gonna make it. And he does."

Jan is a familiar figure around the Genesee Yacht Club, a byproduct of her crewing on *Desire* and her gregarious character when she's hanging out at the modest clubhouse. It is her environment, and Ernie's as well. Charlie, however, finds comfort in the more-moneyed Rochester Yacht Club. Even in non-sailing season, the evenings can roar with conversation as landlocked sailors sit at the bar, ordering food and drinks, waiting for spring to arrive and the day they can get their boats in the water. From the Solings, Charlie had graduated to a J/24, while also spending 24 years crewing on one of the grandest yachts at the club, the 47-foot, black-hulled, Bruce Farr-designed racing boat, *Rampage.* All while sailing up the ladder at the Rochester Yacht Club, with a term as commodore in 2009-'10.

Ernie now belongs to both the Genesee Yacht Club and the Rochester Yacht Club. Everyone on both sides of the docks knows the modest old carpenter. "See that gray shed over there?" says State Supreme Court Justice Kenny Fisher, standing at the front door of the RYC and pointing across the parking lot and docks, now empty for the winter season. "Ernie's there almost every morning, with all the old hands. They get together for coffee."

"He is a landmark in Rochester," Roger Libby says. "Even at the Sodus Bay Yacht Club, the Canandaigua Yacht Club, they know him. You tell them you sailed with Ernie, that opens up a whole 20 minutes of stories."

Roger's got 'em. He and his wife, Diane, are Maine natives. They came to Rochester in the 1970s, twentysomethings recruited as chemical engineers by Eastman Kodak at a time when the photography giant was the heart and business soul of the city. It was after a chance meeting, when their boats were sharing dock space, that Ernie recruited the Libbys to crew with him on *Desire.* It was a relationship that lasted nearly 20 years, the Libbys sailing with Ernie well into the '90s.

"We kind of hit it off," Roger says. "He really became my Rochester father. My father died in '83, and we were like Ernie's kids. We got along like family. We argued like family. When Diane started racing, Evie would even come out. She'd be on *Desire* on Tuesdays, which were not quite as competitive races."

But make no mistake, Roger says. Ernie made it clear why they were out there.

"For 10, 12 years, for small boats under 30 feet, we were the team to beat," he says. "We put more trophies in those two yacht clubs than any other boat. We raced hard, we raced to win. When the race was over, the race was over. We went into the club and had a good time. We didn't debate it."

The Libbys retired to Mars Hill, Maine, in the early part of the new century, as Kodak was tumbling from the city map in a dizzying economic slide of downsizing and planned implosions of deserted buildings. Roger doesn't remember the races with the exacting precision that Ernie shows off, but the feel of those races hasn't left him.

"The ones that really stand out were the Scotch Bonnet light races," Roger says. The ones across the lake to Canada, looping around tiny Scotch Bonnet Island, and then a return to Rochester. "And the ones that were scary, with treacherous thunderstorms and lightning, when the storms were so close you could hear the rigging singing."

The key, Roger adds, was consistency. And crew members knowing their precise roles.

"We would get into tacking duels with another boat owned by … oh, what was his name? Denny Doyle, on *Bangalore*. He had just one large mainsail, so for him to tack was very easy. He would trail right behind us, hoping we'd make a mistake and then he would shoot by us. But we rarely made mistakes.

"I knew the basics of sailing when we first met. Ernie is probably the person who taught me 90 percent of what I know about sailing. He stayed up with technology changes, installing compasses and telltales, then he got LORAN. I used most of the electronics, while he sailed by the seat of his pants, because he was that good. Sometimes things like GPS, on long-distance racing it could be difficult to get Ernie to believe the instruments. You'd tell him we were starting to drift and the winds were changing, but he tended to go with his instincts. He slowly came around to modern technology. It helped us, and his ability to helm the boat and feel it, and my wife's ability to trim the sails.

"I wouldn't trade our relationship for anything in the world. We worked and learned together. He was a family man, down to earth. He'd give you the shirt off his back."

Ernie shared all of his vast life experience with the Libbys. Except, Roger says, "he never talked about the war."

Craig Roth has sailed with Ernie on Wednesdays for the last decade. A decade during which the suddenly scuffed-up Ernie has been held together with bailing wire and spit while he pilots *Desire*. "He holds up great," Craig says. "I'll be amazed when I'm his age if I can do that."

The stories Ernie tells are more than a bonus. With *Desire* not quite the competitive boat that it once was, shooting the breeze as the sails fill with air may now be the point.

"I just enjoy being around him," Craig says. "He's had a lot of experiences, he has a lot of stories. He talks about when he sailed smaller boats. The Sunfish and, I think it was the Snipe. His history in the Navy during World War II." Retired from the Department of Social Services' Fair Hearing Unit, Craig was never in the Navy himself. But his father was, and Craig was born a Navy brat. Perhaps that association brings the service stories out of Ernie.

"He talks about his time in Hawaii," Craig says. While he's on the phone, discussing Ernie, Craig's parrot can be heard in the background, whistling in agreement. "He was a carpenter's mate. He talks about the different ships he was on. The *Saratoga*. But he wasn't on that one long. It took a torpedo and came back to port, and they took Ernie off before it left again."

Saratoga? That's a bit of Ernie's war history that he'd never mentioned. Charlie, too, had never heard Ernie speak of the battle-decorated aircraft carrier. A check of the *Saratoga*'s war record shows that it was supporting the Marine landings on Guadalcanal and, a month after the Battle of Savo Island, was hit by a torpedo from a Japanese submarine. Forced to limp back to Pearl Harbor for repairs, *Saratoga* was very likely the ship that took Ernie back to Hawaii.

Craig is asked about *Vincennes*. Did Ernie ever mention it as they sailed Lake Ontario?

The phone line is silent as Craig ponders the question. "I didn't know," he says after a few seconds, "he was on the *Vincennes*."

Piece by piece, Ernie's story comes together. Like that pile of lumber to which he's fond of referring, a shapeless pile that with some work becomes a boat or a house or a life story.

Steve Lockner, Marilyn's son, the whiskey-drinking Harley guy, tried to put together the story as well. He searched the Internet for photos of

Vincennes, thinking he might be able to get a few on the wall of the local VFW. "They take a picture of every ship when it's being launched," he says. "I was hoping I could find one of those." Marilyn reigned him in. "Ma said, 'Don't bring that up. It gives him nightmares.' "

Perhaps it's because he was in the service as well. But, more than most people around Ernie, Steve seems to have gotten deeper into the story of the old sailor's last night on *Vincennes.* "I was called back up for Desert Storm," Steve says. "Stuck in a tent in the desert, at night, all you could hear were Scud missiles coming down." He and Ernie discussed this. "We'd talk about how you'd listen for the shell fragments to land, so you'd know how close or how far away they were. And he'd say, yeah, he knew what I was talking about."

And then Ernie told of the nightmare sight of water on fire, all around the ship. And the decision he made that he believes saved his life.

More of the story took shape after Charlie heard one of the old sailors at the Rochester Yacht Club describing how he'd just returned from Washington, D.C., with the Rochester chapter of Honor Flights. The national group organizes trips for the rapidly dwindling number of vets – it's estimated 1,000 of them die every day – who want to see the World War II memorial in their final years. "I thought Ernie would enjoy that," Charlie says. Indeed, "He was excited by the idea right away."

Father and son made the journey in the fall of 2009, after Ernie's latest round of knee surgeries had healed. The Rochester chapter, "Maybe 50 vets, each with at least one escort, plus a handful of people as guides," Charlie says, flew into D.C. for dinner, a night in a hotel and a trip to the memorial. Veterans from throughout the country were piled into buses and driven to the site. Although their bodies were sagging with age, these were men of epic stature, witnesses to an event that swept across the entire planet. But the weather was miserable, the rain so heavy that the aging veterans, all likely prime candidates for pneumonia, hardly left their buses. "Ernie was disappointed he wasn't able to get out and look for any of his old shipmates," Charlie says.

Yet rain or not, he'd arrived. Many never would. The World War II memorial estimates 404,800 of Ernie's fellow U.S. servicemen were killed in the war; some estimates are even greater. One section of the memorial is called the Freedom Wall, with 4,048 gold stars, each one representing 100 Americans who died in the war.

By then, Charlie and the family members who had been at that 2008 Thanksgiving dinner had heard a story they'd never dreamed existed. Urged on by family members, Ernie had finally relented, describing what he could, crying through it. Then he was finished. "Please don't ask me to talk about it again," he said afterward. "It gives me nightmares."

"The first shell hit the carpenter's shop and killed a lot of his friends," Charlie recalls of what Ernie told them. "At that time, Ernie was down below. They were all rushed up to the deck to fight fires. Everyone became a fireman. When the call came to abandon ship, they tried to put a lifejacket on him, but he refused."

One can imagine now what was going through Ernie's mind. He was calling on the experiences of his youth. The challenges he had made of himself to swim across Canandaigua Lake. The fearlessness that comes with soaring through the air with a homemade tumbling team during high school. Wrestling with uncertainty while standing on Lock 32 before diving into the canal for the first time. Or, having fallen through the ice and into the canal as a young teenager, turning to the survival instinct that told him he must figure out which way is up in that dark, freezing water, and swim back to that hole, or die.

"The water was on fire," Charlie says. "He didn't want to float around in the middle of that in a life jacket. He dove in and swam as far as he could under water, maybe 100 yards, until he came up on the other side of the fire. And that's how he survived."

Chapter Twenty

The lake is steely gray, the sky a low ceiling of uninspiring clouds, the temperature struggling to reach 50 degrees. Soaring overhead is the new O'Rourke Bridge, named for a Rochester Civil War colonel shot dead at Gettysburg. Below, spread out along the east bank of the Genesee River, is the Genesee Yacht Club. It's a small but cozy clubhouse and a handful of metal-sided buildings, with a 10-year wait for the dock area's 50 berths. But now they're deserted, except for a few seagulls poking at something seemingly interesting near a garbage can, until they scream in disappointment and strut away.

Sailing season is over. This is the final haul-out day. The boats are being moved to the gray-gravel-mud parking area, balanced on their impossibly spindly stands, bundled in bright blue tarps for the winter. Many of the club's 128 member boats are here. Only 13 remain to be plucked from the chilly water on this late-October morning. Ernie likes to hold back *Desire*'s haul out, leaving it to be among this last group. It is his final racing strategy of the season. "The last in, the first out," he says.

The clean winds of sailing have given way to the smells and sounds of diesel engines. Masts have been taken down and laid lengthwise on the boats, which then humbly motor their way into a basin built into the bank of the river. Brown and yellow leaves, and small twigs, float in the basin, crowding into the corners. Just a few hundred yards up river, the steep banks of the Genesee are still alive with a few weeks' brief burst of the leaves' colors. Then they die and fall into the water, dodging among the dead tree branches, meandering slowly downstream. In the contemplative mood cast by the season, and the orderly, almost ceremonial close to sailing, the mind drifts easily to silly allegories of the River Styx and this river of sticks....

But we digress; work is yet to be done. A towering four-wheeled lift is driven over the top of the basin, straddling the boat. Two stout straps are positioned on either side of the keel, and the boat is hauled up. The lift moves the boat away from the basin, stopping over the spot where a forklift or a tractor has set the boat's cradle. More than a few of the owners refer to their boats as "Baby." After the hull is power washed, the boat is set down on its cradle and towed away, and the haul-out crew moves on to the next boat.

The operation is well practiced. "A lot of these guys are retired, they're not working anymore, they spend all week on the haul out," says one of the club members, Gerard Fisher. His boat, *Bebob*, has just come out of the water and now he's helping with the next, *Kraken*. "Last year the average age of the members was 62," Fisher says. "This year it's 63. They're getting new members. But most of them are old." Fisher has about a decade to go before he reaches that average.

At 93, Ernie skews the numbers a bit. He has a green plastic chair sitting at the edge of the activity, but he's not using it much. Instead, he scuttles around in his crab-like walk along the edge of the basin, holding a line or using a boat hook to keep a boat from bumping against the concrete sides. He's not trying to run the show, just staying involved. "He's a great guy," Fisher says. "A lot of these old timers, you put 20 of them in a room and you get 20 different opinions on something. If Ernie walks in the room, you still have 20 opinions. He doesn't say anything unless he thinks you're really screwing up."

Ernie's not saying much this morning. He's too busy conducting reconnaissance. He points to *Kraken*. "He's the same rating as me," he says as *Kraken* hangs in the air. "That'll be my competition next year."

The boats look helpless in the hoist, their privates exposed. Rudders and propellers at the back. Midway up, the keel. A few smaller boats, like *Bebob*, have centerboard keels that crank up inside the boat, just like what Ernie used to install on his Snipes. But most have heavy fixed keels, protruding three or four feet from the bottom of the boat, squares of cast iron with a tapered leading edge, yet blunt like a wood maul. These counterbalance the weight of the mast, and provide enough resistance to keep the boat from sliding sideways in the wind.

Many of the experienced club members are grumbling that today's haul out is going slower than usual. *Freedom*'s mast rolls off the side of the boat and into the basin, and has to be fetched by a crane. Some of the boats aren't quite ready, and the minor delays add up.

Ernie's daughter Jan is also here. *Desire* is out of the water now, and she runs the palm of her hand along the fiberglass hull, where the power washing has left the area below the waterline a dull blue-gray. "I missed a spot there," she says, pointing to a smudge that looks pretty minor. "You miss that mud or grease, it can be a pain in the ass to get off in the spring." She pushes on some tiny blisters beneath the paint on the cast-iron keel, until they pop and bleed water. These imperfections are the size of a ladybug. They will be sanded smooth and the bottom painted after winter recedes.

Ernie doesn't regard the haul out as an end. The seasons are as much a part of sailing as they are to farming. Planning, preparation, anticipation, a fresh start each spring. "You've got something to look forward to," he says. "I know guys who move to Florida, they put their boats in the water, they hardly use them. I know one guy, he told me he would go out once a week, then once a month. Now it's about once a season."

Florida. God's Waiting Room. They probably pipe Vangelis through the speakers there as well, but it sounds more thrilling when you're riding a five-masted clipper ship into the sunset. Ernie says his brother Frank, now 98 years old, was complaining that, when he reached age 95, he could only hit a golf ball 200 yards. Golfing at age 95. Two-hundred yards. Frank's been working for every day he gets, just like Ernie.

But you've also got to be lucky for admission to the Century Club, even if you have to finish the last stretch with a walker. As he talks about his brother retired in Florida, Ernie begins thinking about Tampa Bay, a body of water that he has sailed. "I wasn't impressed," he says. "Even the wind didn't feel right. You've got to watch for buoys, there's a lot of shallow spots. Here, you just go out and go wherever you want."

Frank lives in a fifth-floor apartment in Bradenton, just south of Tampa Bay. Ernie recalls watching from there as a planned detonation took down some of the remains of an overland section of the old Sunshine Skyway bridge. Ernie starts telling a story he read about a guy who was standing on the deck of a 580-foot bulk freighter back in 1980 as it was trying to pass under the Sunshine Skyway in a near-zero-visibility rainstorm. *Summit Venture* crashed into the bridge, and a center section of it buckled and collapsed into the bay. Some of it came down onto the ship as well, where a section with a hatch for maintaining the bridge was fortuitously left unsecured, the opening landing right over the man on the deck. Pure luck. "The guy wasn't even scratched," Ernie says. "A bus landed on its top and everybody was crushed. That was it. Cars went in, they managed to crawl out. So you can't worry about those things."

Well, when you hit 93, you're probably not going to get all of the details right, either. Or perhaps it's simply one of those oft-repeated urban legends. A section of the bridge did land on *Summit Venture,* but no guy on the deck caught a lucky break that morning. Maybe that was another bridge. A bus did plunge into the water, and 26 people in it died. Six cars fell off the bridge, and all nine people in them died. But the driver of a pickup truck that went off the bridge caught a different lucky break. The truck hit *Summit Venture* first, breaking its fall, before it slid into the bay. The guy swam to the surface, the only survivor among those who fell into the water. The fact that he had lived, and the others died, haunted him for the rest of his life.

But Ernie's recollection was pretty close. Perhaps it's not surprising that he'd take an interest in such an incident, later ruled by the Coast Guard and a state grand jury as an Act of God. Fragile human bodies generally lose in calamitous events involving massive amounts of iron and steel and deep water. In reading about the Sunshine Skyway bridge three decades after the collapse, it's striking how some of the details can feel like what might have happened on *Vincennes* on the night that it sank. Narrow escapes from death that certainly matched this one, as the Sunshine Skyway fell into the water: A Buick with four men in it skidded to a stop, the left front wheel 14 inches from where the span had broken off 150 feet above the water.

In the days following the accident, a diver descended some 60 feet to the floor of the bay, drifting through the bridge wreckage and lost cars, and noted how the noise from the collision, and from the bridge falling into the water, seemed to have scared off all of the marine life. Ernie himself remarked on such a phenomena while based in Maui: There were no whales to be seen in those whale-watching waters in the months, more than a year even, after the attack on Pearl Harbor some 111 miles away. Maybe that is also what saved many of the men floating that early morning in Iron Bottom Sound, in a wartime irony: The explosions that tore apart their ships cleared the generally shark-heavy waters.

Perhaps fate, like a surly-looking hitchhiker, is best left in the rear-view mirror, unexamined. Ships sink, spouses die, kids fall through the canal ice and only some of them fight their way back to the surface. Most often, the outcome of these events is out of our control. Outliving everyone around you isn't actually a question of mortality. "It's how you feel," Ernie says, "when your time is up."

If he were still climbing that Mayan pyramid, one step for each year, after 93 years Ernie would have ascended 4,200 steps. Plus another 23 for leap years. "I saw radio," he says. "Television. Jet planes, just to name a few. Super railways. We had railways when I was a kid, but not super railways. And the computer."

The haul out is finished. Ernie has *Desire* positioned right where he wants it. At the front of the line, bow facing the basin, pointing toward next spring. His final racing strategy. Last one in, first one out.

Epilogue

Few of us are allowed the privilege of witnessing a century of life's rich, and inevitably painful, pageant. Ernie Coleman is closing in on that milestone.

He remains a pretty common fellow, as carpenters tend to be. Nevertheless, his friends and family see him as heroic in ways that are difficult to define. Perhaps it's his old-school, hands-on work ethic. But that's a quality we've witnessed in many people who grew up in the hardship of the Great Depression. Perhaps it's his success as a sailor, winning races for decades on Lake Ontario. But other sailors win races. Perhaps it's how he stepped in as the head of a household full of kids blossoming into teenagers and quelled the rebellion. But we've already had *The Brady Bunch*. Perhaps it's his plainspoken manner, or the twinkling devil on his shoulder that still says yes to a scotch on the rocks.

Perhaps it's because Ernie's lived so damn long. When his family threw a 95th birthday party for him in November of 2011, they rented a hall and had to cut off the guest list at about 200. This, despite the fact that Ernie has outlived many of his friends. He's been instructed by his doctors to take it easy now, but it's against the law to tie the guy to a chair. When I stopped by his house one Saturday afternoon in 2010, he was out back, painting the prefabricated tool shed that his family had just purchased for him. When he finished, he sat down in the kitchen and had a glass of red wine.

Ernie is also a hero, although the details were known to few family members, and virtually none of his friends. He was a witness to an epic moment in history that he doesn't talk about. He's filed it away in the place where we put pain, so that we can move on with our lives. He never thinks of himself as a hero in this larger way, although you will likely disagree.

Three chapters in this book have confronted that moment, and there are scattered references elsewhere. Ernie knows they are here. He prefers not to acknowledge them, and he has the right to make that choice. Few of us have ever had to face such a horror. The human psyche is far more fragile than we care to admit.

Most of us hope to live meaningful lives, and have an impact on those closest to us. We probably won't change the course of world events. Yet the stories of people like Ernie are useful in that larger way, because they are the truth. If those truths give us pause before we rush men and women into harm's way, that is good. Or, if those truths simply show a young sailor how to find an elusive breeze on an otherwise peaceful lake, that is good as well.

– JEFF SPEVAK, February 2012

With Ernie Coleman at the helm, another sunset follows *Desire* home.

Photo by Betsy Lawless.

Made in the USA
Lexington, KY
12 May 2012